371
main
The Cooperat

2 1765 0001 6258 9

A Systematic Process for Planning Media Programs

by
JAMES W. LIESENER
Professor
College of Library and Information Services
University of Maryland

WITHDRAWN

American Library Association   Chicago 1976

371, 331
L719L
1976

Library of Congress Cataloging in Publication Data

Liesener, James W   1933-
    A systematic process for planning media programs.

    Bibliography: p.
    1. Media programs (Education)   I. Title.
LB1028.4.L53   658'.91'0278   76-3507

ISBN 0-8389-0176-x

Copyright © 1976 by the American Library Association.
All rights reserved. No part of this publication may be
reproduced in any form without permission in writing from
the publisher, except by a reviewer who may quote brief
passages in a review.

Printed in the United States of America.

CONTENTS

ILLUSTRATIONS

PREFACE

The process, techniques, and conceptual model described herein are the result of efforts, begun in 1968, to conceptualize media programs more systematically and to develop more sophisticated management tools for improving the capability of media personnel to articulate and develop more responsive and effective programs of media services. Some substantial work had been done in librarianship and education to adapt and develop management concepts and techniques, but little had been done to apply and develop these ideas and methods specifically to the management of media programs.[1] This effort, then, is an attempt to adapt and apply some of the ideas and techniques developed in other areas, as well as to develop the additional techniques necessary to provide a reasonably comprehensive and readily usable systematic planning process specifically for media programs.

The initial idea to concentrate on the analysis and conceptualization of media services was provided by the pioneering work of Mary Gaver.[2] However, the impetus to pursue this idea was provided by Edwin E. Olson when he joined the faculty of the College of Library and Information Services at the University of Maryland and involved the author in his research with the development of a generalized library service inventory and service preference scheme. (The basic work in these two approaches was done earlier, however, at the Institute for the Advancement of Medical Communication in Philadelphia, by Richard H. Orr and others, in developing methodologies for planning and managing library services.)[3] The further work, directed by Olson, was an attempt to develop a service inventory appropriate for all kinds of libraries, and the author, as well as a school library task force, worked with other groups (representing other constituencies) to ensure the applicability of the final instrument to the school library situation.[4] This instrument was then used in a statewide survey of library services in Indiana, including school libraries.[5]

The initial development of the technique for determining service preferences and priorities, which is the second technique employed in this work, also began with the work of Orr and continued with Olson in development of the technique for the Indiana survey. This technique, however, was developed further in an experimental educational project with the National Agricultural Library before its adaptation for media programs.[6]

The next major phase in the development of this planning process and instrumentation was made possible by the Division of Library Development and Services, Maryland State Department of Education, which funded a project the author directed from July 1971 to August 1972. The objective was to develop the methodology for identifying and analyzing the resource requirements and costs of the entire range of alternative media service outputs, as well as the methodology for determining the needs for services or the relative value of alternative services in any school program. The project also involved the substantial adaptation and development of the previously mentioned techniques specifically for school media programs, as well as the development of the two additional techniques and instrumentation for identifying and collecting the necessary data and for organizing and analyzing these data in order to facilitate program decision making. A number of school personnel and other individuals provided significant input into this project, but the Montgomery County public schools (Maryland) in particular provided the major "test bed" for the development of the techniques and instruments in this phase. The report of this project was disseminated to all state school library supervisors as well as to numerous other individuals in the field, and their favorable responses, suggestions, and criticisms provided the impetus for the next phase of development, as well as many ideas for substantive changes.[7]

The final phase of development involved the elaboration of the planning process into a systematic and step-by-step process, as well as the further testing and revision of the techniques and instrumentation employed in the process. Brief descriptions of the process were published to solicit additional feedback[8] and the process and techniques were tested by a number of practitioners, as well as on a broader scale through a series of workshops.

Thirty-three workshops, varying from one day to two weeks, and in some cases distributed over a longer period of time as implementation of the process occurred, were conducted in the following thirteen states from October 1972 to June 1975: Colorado, Florida, Illinois, Maryland, Michigan, New Jersey, New York, North Carolina, Ohio, Oregon, Texas, Virginia, and Wisconsin. These workshops were sponsored by universities, state education agencies, professional associations and school districts, and have involved over 900 school building, district, and state media personnel as well as school administrators.

The workshop participants were introduced to the process and given opportunities to apply the techniques, in many cases in their own school situations as well as in the workshops, and then were asked to provide feedback. This testing and feedback resulted in another extensive revision of the four instruments, which was completed in January 1974—with some final subsequent testing in workshops and by individual practitioners resulting in a great many suggestions regarding the application of the process and techniques (which are incorporated in the following narrative).[9]

It should be stated that in spite of the considerable testing of the process and techniques in the workshops and independently by a number of individual practitioners, it was not possible to do a number of large-scale and carefully controlled pilot projects so as to thoroughly test all aspects of this process and the consequences of its application. Such a test can be made in the future, along with the development of norms for comparison of media programs. The further application and development of this process and techniques for district and regional media programs, as well as an exploratory service output survey, is just being completed in a project funded by the Division of Instructional Resources of the Texas Education Agency.[10] It is hoped that this process can also be applied to state media agencies and services so that the entire hierarchy of media services can be viewed and planned in a systematic manner.

It is impossible to acknowledge all the individuals who made significant contributions in the various phases of this work, but the author wishes to express particular appreciation to the following:

Dr. Richard H. Orr and others at the Institute for Medical Communication, who did the original work for some of the techniques developed by the author for application specifically to planning media programs;

Dr. Edwin E. Olson, who continued at the College of Library and Information Services the work which was begun at the Institute for Medical Communication and who stimulated the author to adapt these ideas for school media programs;

Mae I. Graham, former Assistant Director, Division of Library Development and Services, Maryland State Department of Education, who provided the impetus and inspiration for the significant middle phase of the development of the planning process and also served as a consultant, and Nettie B. Taylor, Assistant State Superintendent and Director of the division, who made this phase possible by providing the funding;

The staff of the Montgomery County public schools (Maryland) and particularly Nancy Walker, Director, Department of Educational Media and Technology, and her staff, who provided a test bed for the development of this process as well as invaluable assistance and information;

Karen M. Levitan, doctoral candidate and co-author of the report of the middle phase of the development, whose keen interest and effort contributed significantly to the final product, and Dr. Donald H. Kraft,

Assistant Professor, who freely contributed his expertise in operations research as well as his enthusiasm, throughout all phases of development, and Dr. Margaret E. Chisholm, former Dean of the College of Library and Information Services, who provided a constant supporting interest as well as consultant assistance and a sabbatical leave which provided the necessary time at a critical stage;

The sponsors and participants of the workshops, as well as all students and practitioners who contributed so much throughout the various stages of development and without whose help in providing information, suggestions, and critical reactions the end result may not have been functional;

And Edie Liesener for freely providing editorial and production assistance as well as consulting assistance throughout all phases of development.

NOTES

1. An early and important exception was the following work, which represented an application of a number of significant management concepts to program planning as well as an effort to provide the instrumentation necessary for implementation: Frances Henne, Ruth Ersted, and Alice Lohrer, *A Planning Guide for the High School Library Program* (American Library Assn., 1951).

2. Mary V. Gaver and Milbrey Jones, "Secondary Library Services: A Search for Essentials," *Teachers College Record* 68:200–10 (Dec. 1966); Mary V. Gaver, "Services in Secondary School Media Centers: A Second Appraisal," *School Libraries* 20:15–21 (Fall 1970); and idem, *Services of Secondary School Media Centers: Evaluation and Development* (American Library Assn., 1971).

3. Richard H. Orr and others, "Development and Methodologic Tools for Planning and Managing Library Services: I. Project Goals and Approach," *Bulletin of the Medical Library Association* 56:235–40 (July 1968); idem, "Development of Methodologic Tools for Planning and Managing Library Services: III. Standardized Inventories of Library Services," *Bulletin of the Medical Library Association* 56:380–403 (Oct. 1968); and Edwin E. Olson, "Quantitative Approaches to Assessment of Library Service Functions," in James A. Ramey, ed., *Impact of Mechanization on Libraries and Information Centers: Fifth Annual National Collo-* quium on Information Retrieval (Information Interscience, 1968), p. 97–113.

4. Edwin E. Olson, "Development of a General Inventory of Library User Services: Description of Project February 1, 1969 to December 31, 1969," mimeographed (College of Library and Information Services, University of Maryland, 1970).

5. Edwin E. Olson, *Survey of User Service Policies in Indiana Libraries and Information Centers,* Indiana Library Studies Report no. 10 (Indiana State Library, 1970), and James W. Liesener and Edwin E. Olson, "Survey of User Services in Indiana School Libraries," *Hoosier School Libraries* 8:7–9 (Summer 1969).

6. Edwin E. Olson and James W. Liesener, *An Experimental Educational Program in Library and Information Services: Report no. 1* (College of Library and Information Services, University of Maryland, 1971), p. 15–32 and 109–24.

7. James W. Liesener and Karen M. Levitan, *A Process for Planning School Media Programs: Defining Service Outputs, Determining Resource and Operational Requirements, and Estimating Program Costs* (College of Library and Information Services, University of Maryland, 1972).

8. James W. Liesener, "A Planning Process for School Library/Media Programs," in David R. Bender, ed., *Issues in Media Management* (Maryland State Department of Education, Division of Li-

brary Development and Services, 1973), p. 31–44; idem, "The Development of a Planning Process for Media Programs," *School Media Quarterly* 1:278–87 (Summer 1973); and Donald H. Kraft and James W. Liesener, "An Application of a Cost-Benefit Approach to Program Planning: School Media Programs," in *Proceedings of the American Society for Information Science* (American Society for Information Science, 1973), p. 116–17.

9. James W. Liesener, *Planning Instruments for School Library/Media Programs.* These instruments are distributed by the Student Supply Store, University of Maryland, College Park, Md. 20742.

10. James W. Liesener, *District and Regional Learning Resource (Media) Programs: A Systematic Planning Process and Exploratory Survey of Services* (Texas Education Agency, 1975).

CHAPTER 1

A Framework for Systematic Program Planning

Development of a planning process and techniques specifically for media program management must obviously incorporate some conception of the particular role or function that media programs are intended to fulfill. It is possible to conceive of the media program in many quite different ways; however, in this context the function or mission of the media specialist or program is viewed as an organized attempt to resolve the mediation problem, which can be characterized as indicated in figure 1. This role is defined as the provision of a program of services for mediating or facilitating the interaction between clients and information or media in order to achieve learning objectives. The traditional distinction between library and audiovisual roles and activities is not functional in this context; rather, both dimensions are seen as totally interrelated and inherent in this conception of media programs.

The problems we confront in attempting to perform this role or mission are considerable and can be considered as constraints on our capacity for carrying out our function adequately. For example, our ability to identify and assess the entire range of information alternatives available, on the one hand, and the terribly complex and varied client needs on the other, in order to provide the most efficacious match, is severely limited by lack of adequate techniques and methods, as well as by time and other resources.

Probably the part of this problem that has received the least attention, however, is the decision process employed by the media specialist in dealing with the problem. How do you make decisions when faced with this kind of dilemma? How do you decide what you are going to do and what you are not going to do, and how do you justify this? What is the best way to utilize the limited resources you have for the maximum effect?

A number of responses are possible. The most common is simply to respond to demands as they arise; however, this almost inevitably results in haphazard and inconsistent service and, frequently, very inefficient and

1

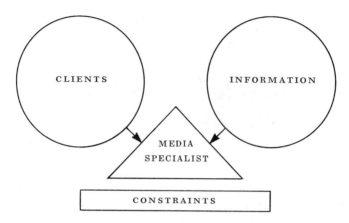

FIG. 1. The mediation problem

ineffective utilization of time and resources. An alternative response, and obviously the one promoted here, is concerted and systematic program planning and evaluation, using what we can of such management techniques as PPBS[1] and systems analysis. However, we have not progressed very far in terms of developing our capability in applying these techniques to school media program planning and managing, in spite of considerable efforts to develop these techniques for educational planning and managing in general.[2]

Pressures for Change

A number of factors have coalesced to intensify the need for a substantial change in the planning behavior of the media specialist. Extreme competition for scarce resources, pervasive concern with accountability, and pressure to apply management techniques (such as PPBS) have exposed the inadequacies of our planning, data-collection, and evaluation procedures in managing media programs. Our traditional minimal involvement in the budgeting process has seriously handicapped our ability and opportunity to oppose arbitrary cuts, to articulate program needs, and to influence resource allocations. The vague generalities and faith we have relied on to document our contribution to (and value in) the educational process are in severe contrast to the systematic and detailed evidence that is demanded for program justification and accountability.

In addition to these pressures, a number of other factors, directly related to media programs, also demand improved management and planning behavior. Media programs have rapidly increased in scale and complexity and can no longer be managed out of one's hip pocket, so to speak. The changes that have occurred in curriculum reform, with the emphasis on individualization and independent study, have stimulated a quantum jump in the needs for information and materials—requiring, also, advanced diagnosis of these needs, since no information system is adequate to respond to these needs simply on demand. The increased alternatives in terms of materials and equipment also require greater advance knowledge of needs and greater judgment in selection.

The literature is resplendent with articles on accountability and the necessity for applying techniques such as PPBS in the educational sector. Notably lacking, however, are concrete suggestions for overcoming some of the very serious problems of implementing, in a social institution such as education, management techniques which were developed in an entirely different context—where, for example, it was easier to determine measurable outputs and resulting payoffs or benefits. A number of more reasonable and responsible presentations of the value and feasibility of these approaches have appeared in the literature, such as the book cited earlier by Stephen J. Knezevich dealing with education, an article by Willard Fazar[3] treating the applications in libraries generally, and particularly Robert Wedgeworth's excellent description of current budgetary planning in school media centers and the potential value and problems in applying PPBS to school media programs.[4] One of Wedgeworth's recommendations directly supports the approach taken here:

> Since there are some indications that state and local governments are increasingly adopting PPBS, it behooves librarians to identify the weak points and suggest modifications to the system before it is forced upon them. Perhaps by developing interim budgeting procedures which embrace some of the principles of PPBS, school media centers can improve their position in the budgeting process and, at the same time, prepare for more modern budget systems. A model for these procedures might be helpful in articulating these advantages.[5]

It seems quite clear that the initial need is not more admonitions and rhetoric but adaptation and development of more sophisticated management and planning methods specifically applied to school media programs so that media specialists can significantly improve their effectiveness in the program planning and budgeting process. The growth and development of media programs and, in a number of circumstances, the very survival of media programs could be at stake.

Response to the Problem

The approach in beginning to develop improved planning tools for media specialists was to take the concepts and methods available from other contexts and adapt and develop them for school media programs. The result was intended to include not only a description of a planning model but the actual techniques and instruments necessary for practitioners to readily use and implement these techniques. It was felt that the less adaptation and development that is necessary for the individual practitioner, the greater the chance that implementation could and would occur. Involvement in this development of state education agencies and media and administrative personnel in school systems was considered essential to ensure the validity and applicability of the end result. However, this participation by potential users, as well as by individuals in responsible leadership positions, was also felt to be very important to help legitimize and therefore increase the receptivity and chances of acceptance by practitioners of this new approach, which would initially appear strange and cumbersome.

A word of caution should be expressed about the criteria or qualities which should be incorporated in the techniques. Our "credibility" in education has been seriously hurt by our too frequent practice of portraying, as new panaceas, ideas which sound promising but are untested and undeveloped. This danger can be substantially reduced if the qualities or requirements indicated in figure 2 are carefully considered and effected.[6] Obviously, however, it is neither easy nor simple to accommodate all of these dimensions equally. A serious effort was made to develop tools which in most cases are practicable and suitable for self-application by practitioners, without the necessity of hiring costly consultants, but this was not taken to the extreme of destroying the reliability and validity or utility of the information derived from the application of the techniques in order to achieve simplicity.

As a result, at least some initial orientation is necessary through reading this description and/or initial training in an in-service workshop or in the basic professional preparation of the media specialist. Some quantification to facilitate greater precision and detailed analysis was essential—but nothing more than the most basic arithmetical skills and ability to use a simple hand calculator (because of the limited mathematical preparation of most media specialists). Very basic systems analysis and costing techniques were employed so that the process could be applied or easily adapted to any media program and still return comparable and reliable results, as well as reflect system- or district-level supporting or supplementary services where appropriate. Another desirable result of taking this basic approach is that the planning process, as developed specifically for media programs, is

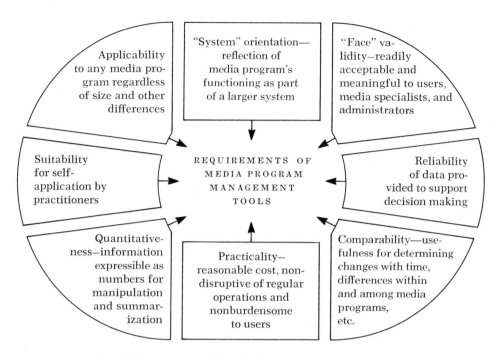

FIG. 2. Requirements of media program management tools

compatible with or easily translated into the accountability or program planning and budgeting schemes that are evolving in many school systems.

With this in mind, the objective was to develop a systematic process and techniques for addressing the following program planning questions:

1. *What,* specifically, is a media program in terms of functions performed for the client (students, teachers, and other school staff) and *how* can this program be communicated effectively?
2. Because resources are always limited, what services are most important or what mix of services is optimal for a given set of local conditions?
3. *Who* determines what is most important for a given set of conditions and *how* is this determination made?
4. What alternative operations and resource allocations are possible to provide a given mix of services? What are the costs and what is the optimal use of resources so as to achieve as much of the desirable as is feasible?

5. How can clients be involved in the planning process in order to increase understanding as well as use of the services provided?

The first step in developing the process and techniques to address these questions was to characterize the media program in terms of a basic systems model. This was done in order (1) to differentiate as discretely as possible the various program components and (2) to reflect as clearly as possible the specific relationships between the component parts. Another objective in this approach was to facilitate means and ends distinctions. Possibly our greatest problem is our failure to clearly distinguish our ends —what we are trying to accomplish—from our means—the resources we have and the operations we perform—to achieve our ends.

Current descriptions of media program services or outputs are very superficial and inadequate, even in such sources as *Media Programs: District and School.*[7] The best current description of media program outputs (although not characterized as such), which attempts to express output in terms of media services, is the questionnaire developed by Mary V. Gaver.[8] However, even Gaver's extensive list does not express the total range and level of potential services in terms of functions performed for the user or with the detail and conceptual coherence necessary to identify and relate the specific resource and operational requirements for the delivery of specified services. This lack of an adequate means for specifying media program outputs is probably the greatest obstacle in the application of more modern planning and program-justification techniques in the development of media programs. Media specialists have been so preoccupied with considerations of quantities of materials and other resources without being able to clearly relate them to a program of specific services to users. The emphasis has been on *means*, on what media centers *have*, rather than on *ends*, what is *done* for users—which is the output of media centers rather than the input or operational means necessary to deliver services. This same inadequacy has reinforced the reliance on subjectively derived quantitative standards to justify the need for program resources. Because these standards cannot be specifically related to service outputs or clearly demonstrable user benefits, this approach for identifying and justifying requests for resources is no longer viable.[9]

A more effective method for planning and budgeting must be able to clearly distinguish between ends and means or, in systems terms, between inputs and outputs, and be able to show the direct relationship between them. The basic model for facilitating these distinctions is shown in figure 3. User services—program outputs or ends—must be defined as clearly and elaborately as possible. This is necessary to differentiate ends, or user services, as distinctly as possible from means, resources, and operations,

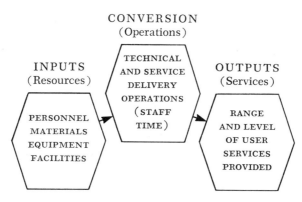

FIG. 3. Media program model

but also so that the specific resource and operational requirements of each specific user service can be made explicit. It is then necessary to identify the specific amounts and variety of raw materials (resources) required for each service output, as well as the specific allocation of staff time (conversion) for performing the various operations and routines necessary to transform the raw materials into services delivered to users. For example, the most traditional library service, provision of materials, involves considerable staff time (conversion) in selecting, acquiring, organizing, and making available (or actually delivering to users) books and other materials (inputs) before use by students and teachers (outputs) can occur.

Conceiving of the media program in this fashion fosters an ends orientation, permits planning to begin with assessment of the relative value or priority of the various service alternatives, and provides the rationale for determining the optimal use of present resources and the need—as well as the justification—for additional resources. Provision of media services is not an end in itself, however, but must be viewed in the broader context of the goals of the embedding institution. The relative value of the alternative service outputs and the requisite resources and operations in effecting these service outputs must therefore be assessed, ultimately, from the perspective of their contribution to the achievement of learning outcomes. This relationship is depicted in figure 4, which also indicates that this contribution occurs both indirectly (by the provision of services to teachers in support of their instructional activities) and directly (by the provision of services to students).

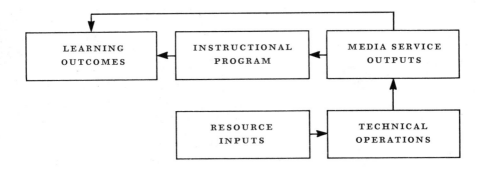

Fig. 4. Media program accountability model

Our current capability for determining the relative value of alternative media services on the basis of objective evidence of direct contribution to the achievement of learning outcomes is at an extremely primitive level, to say the very least. The assessment of relative values in planning and justifying a program of services is imperative, however, if accountability for results and not only internal efficiency is to be achieved. The planning process described in succeeding chapters therefore incorporates a technique for assessing the relative values or needs for services, at least in a relatively objective and systematic fashion, in order to provide a results-oriented basis for program planning. The approach represents a direct confrontation of instructional and learning intentions and behavior and the diagnosis of the resulting media service needs and alternative service responses. This approach does not require the typical extreme emphasis on what so frequently represents only rhetorical manipulation in the generation of explicit goals and objectives as a preliminary planning activity. However, clarification of the instructional and media program goals and objectives is an inevitable result of the interactive process employed. The process focuses on the collective development of explicit and agreed-upon service priorities and performance targets that are directly related to whatever kind and level of goal and objective formulation is locally suitable and feasible. The end result, however, represents a detailed and effective analysis and expression by the clients and media staff of instructional and learning needs for explicitly defined media services (objectives) and in terms that can be readily translated into measurable service behavior.[10]

NOTES

1. Acronym for the "planning-programming-budgeting system" developed by the Rand Corporation and installed and popularized by the U.S. Department of Defense: an integrated and systematic system to facilitate planning and decision making.

2. An excellent introduction to this subject and an analysis of current applications in education is Stephen J. Knezevich, *Program Budgeting (PPBS): A Resource Allocation Decision System for Education* (McCutchan Publishing Corp., 1973). The most extensive review of the work on performance measures and the implications for media programs is Evelyn H. Daniel, "Performance Measurement for School Libraries," in Melvin J. Voight and Michael H. Harris, eds., *Advances in Librarianship,* vol. 6. (To be published by Academic Pr. in 1976).

3. Willard Fazar, "Program Planning and Budgeting Theory," *Special Libraries* 60:423–33 (Sept. 1969).

4. Robert Wedgeworth, "Budgeting for School Media Centers," *School Libraries* 20:29–36 (Spring 1971).

5. Ibid., p. 34.

6. These basic methodological considerations and criteria were adapted from those developed at the Institute for the Advancement of Medical Communication and are discussed in more detail in the following articles: Richard H. Orr and others, "Development of Methodologic Tools for Planning and Managing Library Services: I. Project Goals and Approach," *Bulletin of the Medical Library Association* 56:236 (July 1968), and Richard H. Orr, "Measuring the Goodness of Library Services: A General Framework for Considering Quantitative Measures," *Journal of Documentation* 29:328–30 (Sept. 1973).

7. American Association of School Librarians and Association for Educational Communication and Technology, *Media Programs: District and School* (American Library Assn., 1975).

8. Mary V. Gaver, *Services of Secondary School Media Centers: Evaluation and Development* (American Library Assn., 1971), p. 123–29.

9. An excellent analysis of the inadequacies of the use of standards is Allan Blackman, "The Meaning and Use of Standards," in Henrik L. Blum and others, *Health Planning: Notes on Comprehensive Planning for Health* (School of Public Health, University of California [Berkeley], 1969), p. 4.33–4.43.

10. For additional suggestions on goal and objective formulation see Ernest R. DeProspo and Alan R. Samuels, "A Program Planning and Evaluation Self Instructional Manual," in James W. Liesener, ed., *Media Program Evaluation in an Accountability Climate: Proceedings of the AASL Special Program, San Francisco, June 29, 1975* (American Library Assn., 1976).

CHAPTER 2

The Planning Process

Planning is viewed here as a process of incorporating a variety of activities and dimensions. The goals and objectives of the embedding institution, the school and its instructional program, must be articulated in order to facilitate the formulation and integration of the goals and objectives of the media program. The relative value of the alternative programs or services must be calculated and evaluated in terms of the identified needs of the local program and client groups. The means for accomplishing these program or service alternatives (the staff and the other resources required) must be determined and considered in relation to the current and projected availability and capability of these resources. The manner and method in which these planning activities are performed are critical.

The goals and objectives, program responses, and operational and resource requirements must be analyzed and expressed in such a way that relationships are clear and well defined and in a manner which facilitates systematic programming or implementation, as well as continuous evaluation of performance and results. Effective and appropriate interaction between clients, administrators, and program staff is a key ingredient, and must be incorporated throughout the planning process in order to achieve the communication necessary to develop client and administrative awareness and support, assess changing needs, and stimulate feedback.

The process for planning, evaluating, and communicating media programs (described in the following paragraphs) attempts to integrate the various components and activities of program planning into a system of nine steps. Performance of the various steps is not necessarily always sequential but may be implemented in many different ways as well as in parts. Implementation of the process, as well as a detailed discussion of each technique, will be dealt with in later chapters.

Media Program Planning Process

STEP 1: DEFINITION OF PROGRAM OUTPUT ALTERNATIVES

TECHNIQUE: *"Inventory of School Library/Media Center Services"*

The very important objective in this step is to develop a consistent, comprehensive, and coherent conception of a media program which delineates the entire range of potential services in terms of functions performed from the user's viewpoint. These media program outputs must be clearly identified in terms of the range and depth or extent of the services provided for the user and explicitly distinguished from resources or operational elements. The "Inventory of School Library/Media Center Services," developed for this purpose (see appendix A), is frequently duplicated and used without adaptation, therefore eliminating step 1 of the process. However, the importance of this instrument should not be underestimated since it is the key to the other instruments and is used as a major vehicle for increasing clients' awareness of media services and determining media program objectives and services. There is little or no current consensus on many of the terms and therefore the "Inventory of School Library/Media Center Services" should be carefully reviewed, at least for terminology changes which may be necessary in the given situation. Care should be exercised, however, so that the basic purpose and conceptual integrity of the instrument (as explained in chapters 1 and 3) is maintained.

The exhaustive list of potential or alternative user outputs or services is essential because preliminary or intuitive judgments regarding what is and is not appropriate or necessary or feasible in a particular situation are not very reliable within our present knowledge and can easily be biased. Also, services which may not be currently feasible may become feasible if enough interest and support are generated. The opportunities for educating clients about media services and obtaining user input on preferred services, regardless of current offerings, also require an initial and exhaustive list of alternative services. The natural inclination here—and a danger—is to greatly reduce and thus oversimplify the instrument and thereby diminish or destroy its educational utility and its usefulness in assessing needs and establishing priorities.

After extensive testing with clients, particularly teachers, the predominant reaction after the initial reaction to the size of the instrument was that the value of the "Inventory of School Library/Media Center Services," in terms of increasing awareness regarding the media program and services, was very significant and the detail was essential to developing this increased understanding. The development of a clear understanding of the media program and its user services on the part of the media staff, clients, and school administrators is undoubtedly the most essential factor in program development and planning. Therefore the instrument or vehicle that is used to conceptualize and articulate the media program is the most important (and basic) step in beginning systematic program planning. To oversimplify at this point and therefore reinforce the naive and grossly inadequate perceptions of the media program which currently prevail would be a most serious mistake.

STEP 2: SURVEY OF PERCEPTIONS OF CURRENT SERVICES

> TECHNIQUE: *Survey of Staff and a Representative Sample of Clients Who Use the "Inventory of School Library/Media Center Services"*

The objective in this step is twofold: first, to carefully assess the current level of staff and client understanding or perception of services currently offered and, second, to begin the process of educating clients by increasing their awareness of the entire range of potential services as well as correcting misconceptions regarding current services. In addition to the primary objectives, the intent is also to increase the involvement of clients in systematic program assessment and planning to establish or reinforce a client and service-oriented posture on the part of the media program.

The "Inventory of School Library/Media Center Services" was constructed in the form of a survey instrument so that it could be used in this step to survey clients and staff. Respondents are asked to complete the form by indicating which specific services they *perceive* that the media center provides or does not provide. Since the "Inventory" is an exhaustive list of services, it confronts the respondent with a systematic array of the potential services, expressed in terms of functions performed for the user, that *could* be provided by a media center. An explanation should be given indicating the purpose of the survey, and also that there are no right or wrong answers since the intent is simply to identify current perceptions of offered services so that misconceptions can be identified and a program developed to correct them.

If one were only concerned with assessing the current level of understanding of the services offered, a relatively small sample of students, teachers, and administrative staff could be used. However, because the educational objective is the more important objective, a much larger sample—or the entire population—is surveyed to achieve this and only a sample of the responses is analyzed to achieve the assessment objective.

The most common pattern is to include all media staff, teachers and administrative staff, and a random sample of between 10 and 20 percent of the students. The instrument is not intended to be used with students below the middle school level (grade six) since this would require simplification to the degree that the validity of the results would be highly questionable. With students who have been selected for the sample but who have reading problems, the instrument must be read to them and their responses recorded on the form or on an answer sheet, if one is used. It is important to include users as well as non-users in the sample in order to achieve an accurate and complete picture of the awareness of media services.

The media staff is first surveyed and any inconsistencies are resolved. This frequently results in development of an overall set of policies for the entire program of services, as well as a more consistent interpretation and implementation of the service policies by all media staff. The media staff responses are then compared to the tabulations of the responses from the teachers (possibly subdivided by grade level or department), students, and administrators. This analysis is usually represented in terms of percent of agreement between the responses of the media staff and the different groups of respondents. These results can then be analyzed to reveal an accurate and in-depth picture of the current understanding and misunderstanding of current service offerings, specific areas where communication of services has been ineffective and needs improvement, and inconsistencies in perceptions and performance of services by various staff members. Reporting back to clients the results of the survey can then be combined with a clarification of the service policies in user terms and an in-service or instructional program aimed at the specific areas and groups where misunderstandings and misconceptions have been identified.

After conducting a number of surveys of this type, it appears that an agreement of 50 percent between the media specialists and the clients is quite good. It is also apparent that some areas are better understood than others; for example, the more negative aspects, such as circulation restrictions, are much more consistently understood than the whole range of other services. This emphasizes that our communication efforts do not seem to have been very effective in the past, improvement is critical, and a beginning can be made with the approach suggested in this step.

In some cases the survey is used only with individuals who are to participate in step 3 and therefore must have initial familiarity with the "Inventory of School Library/Media Center Services." However (unless there is no alternative), this is not recommended since the objectives in this step are absolutely essential to planning and developing an optimally effective media program.

STEP 3: DETERMINATION OF SERVICE PREFERENCES AND PRIORITIES
IN RELATION TO LOCAL NEEDS

TECHNIQUE: *Group Session of Clients and Staff, Using the "Form
for Determining Preferences for School Library/Media
Center Services"*

In step 2 the focus was on clarifying and assessing the level of understanding of currently offered services and service policies. Step 3 focuses
not on what *is* but what *should be* in terms of calculation of the relative
value or need for the various service alternatives in relation to the specific
needs and objectives of the clients and instructional program in a given
situation.

The decision regarding what will be done or what services will be provided in a given situation is rarely calculated very carefully and is seldom
performed consistently. This very likely contributes considerably to user
frustration and confusion regarding the media program. Resources are
always limited (although relatively so), and careful planning is necessary
if the greatest user benefit is to be derived from the utilization of available
resources. Services must also be limited to what can be provided reliably
and dependably if user benefit—rather than frustration—is to be achieved.

The process for identifying needs and determining responsive service
priorities, as recommended here, assumes that our capability to perform
valid needs assessment in a strictly rational and objective fashion is inadequate. It is also assumed that authoritarian or subjective judgments by
the media specialist alone, regarding service offerings, are inappropriate
as well as inadequate. What is recommended is a combination of political
and management techniques directed at establishing collective decision
making involving clients and media staff. It is suggested that systematic
client and administrative participation in program decisions is not only
likely to lead to better program decisions but substantially increases the
likelihood that the services will be used and the program effectively sup-
ported. This also tends to provide a check on the subjectivity of the media
specialist in fashioning a program, as well as provide the client the opportunity, if not the right, for a "say" in the determination of the services
they receive. In political terms, this approach not only responds to the
need to address the traditional authority, the administrative hierarchy,
but also attempts to organize and mobilize a constituency of clients in
support of the program and its needs in contributing to achieving the goals
and objectives of the institution.

The technique and process employed (see appendix B and chapter 4)
to assess needs and establish priorities involves the selection of a representative group of clients, who have participated in step 2, to participate

with the media staff in translating the educational goals and objectives as well as considerations of instructional strategies and student characteristics into specific media service needs and relative priorities. The instrument is an abbreviation or outline of the services delineated in the "Inventory of School Library/Media Center Services." The participants are required, first individually and then as a group, to assign specific and relative values to the various service alternatives in accord with their consideration of the importance or need for these service alternatives in relation to the factors indicated previously. The result is a consensus on the relative value of the alternative services in relation to the special needs of the given program and clients, as interpreted by the clients themselves in cooperation with the media staff. These, then, become the objectives and priorities for the media program and are later translated into specific program performance targets.

In addition to a systematic and consensual assessment of service needs and priorities with clear documentation, this process stimulates a number of valuable by-products. The interaction and the resultant mutual understanding of instructional program activities and requisite media services which occurs is undoubtedly a valuable end in and of itself. The increase in service appetites, which inevitably occurs as a result of greater awareness of services and the utility of these services, is also a very desirable outcome and very much in the media specialist's as well as the client's self-interest.

The by-product most frequently overlooked, but which represents a considerable shift in strategy, is the development of an informed client constituency. An informed and supportive constituency, combined with systematic documentation of needs, is certainly a better strategy than the previously myopic and overly simplistic approach of attempting to impress and influence administrators with our good intentions and with vague generalities and assertions regarding the value of media programs.

STEP 4: ASSESSMENT OF RESOURCE AND OPERATIONAL REQUIREMENTS
        OF SERVICES

        TECHNIQUE: *Data Collection and Analysis, Using the "School Library/Media Program Data Collection Guide"*

To determine what is feasible in a given situation it is necessary to identify the resource and operational requirements of providing specific services at certain use levels. This is possibly the most problematic area in planning. The data we presently have available are not really very useful; so it is a matter of collecting the data and in such a way as to be able to relate them to a specific service output. Particularly troublesome are the allocation of staff time, the documentation of the kind and amount required for a specific service, and the documentation of the delivery of some categories of service outputs.

An instrument for identifying and recording the data to be collected in this step was designed to suggest the kinds of data to be collected and a sampling approach to collecting them (see appendix C and chapter 5). What is required is identification of all the operations involved in performing each service and estimations by taking a number of samples of the time it takes each staff member to perform each operation. A gross estimate can then be calculated of the amount of staff time involved in delivering a specific service at a given use level—for example, the number of times provided or the number of items provided. Records of the amounts of other resources, such as materials, equipment, and supplies required to provide a service at a given use level, must also be kept in order to calculate the total resource requirements of delivering services. The critical factor is to gather the data in such a way as to be able to identify all of the resources, including the staff time required for providing each user service.

Determination of the resource and operational requirements and costs for specific services in the local situation is essential, and there are no generalized resource requirement and cost estimates which can be utilized, particularly in the area of staff time. Some resource cost figures that are generally available can be used, but considerable local data collection is unavoidable.

STEP 5: DETERMINATION OF COSTS OF PREFERRED SERVICES
        AND/OR CURRENT SERVICES

TECHNIQUE: *Completion of "School Library/Media Program Costing Matrix" for Current Service Costs and/or Preferred Service Costs*

The data collected in step 4 can now be used, along with salary and materials cost figures, to determine first the expenditures for current service offerings and, secondly, the estimated costs of the preferred mix of services at an estimated use or output level. The instrument that has been developed to facilitate these calculations requires only the most basic arithmetic skills and is designed to amalgamate (in one place) all the various program data (see appendix D and chapter 6). This working document also provides the media specialist the basis for a variety of analyses of the program and the source of the various kinds of data that can be used for reporting to administrators and clients.

STEP 6: CALCULATION OF PROGRAM CAPABILITY

> TECHNIQUE:
> A. *Comparison of Current Available Resources with Resource Costs of Preferred Services*
> B. *Calculation of Range and Level of Preferred Services Currently Feasible with Resources Available*

The results of these comparisons and calculations will clearly reflect how many, and to what extent, preferred services can be provided with available resources. In other words, specific and measurable program or performance targets can be established. This also provides a precise picture of what additional resources or funds are necessary to expand service offerings to any desired level.

STEP 7: COMMUNICATION OF PREFERRED SERVICES CURRENTLY FEASIBLE TO TOTAL CLIENT GROUP

> TECHNIQUE: *Group Presentation of Abbreviated "Form for Determining Preferences for School Library/Media Center Services," Indicating Current Capability*

The objective here is to inform clients about which of these preferred services will and will not be provided, due to resource limitations. This should provide a clear picture (probably for the first time) of what clients can and cannot expect from the media program, and why. It also stimulates requests and support for more resources in order to provide the additional services they feel they absolutely need. However, this expression of need and support is now directed at the administration, and is more constructive since it is framed in terms of specific needs for specific services and with the understanding that the problem is the need for additional resources to provide these services rather than disinterest or unwillingness on the part of the media staff. This effort should certainly help to promote the attitude of the media program as a joint endeavor of mutual concern and benefit to all the parties involved.

STEP 8: REALLOCATION OF RESOURCES AND IMPLEMENTATION OF CHANGES
IN OPERATIONS TO PROVIDE THE RANGE AND LEVEL OF
SERVICES SELECTED

> TECHNIQUE: *Use of Information from the*
> A. *"School Library/Media Program Data Collection Guide"*
> B. *"Form for Determining Preferences for School
>   Library/Media Center Services"*
> C. *"School Library/Media Program Costing Matrix"
>   to Determine Resource Reallocations and Operational
>   Changes Needed*

There may be technical problems in some systems in making the reallocations necessary to implement the preferred services. Because of the use
of formula budgeting and restrictions on budget transfers—for example,
using money allocated for materials for part-time staff—it may not be
possible to shift the resources (for example) to concentrate more heavily
on labor-intensive services such as reference, rather than on materials-
intensive kinds of services. However, this documentation for more flexibility in budgeting can be a beginning toward influencing the changes in
system budgeting and accounting procedures necessary to make it possible
to adapt and tailor media programs in response to individual and possibly
unique instructional program needs.

It is also possible at this point to establish specific and measurable program performance targets—for example, for the next academic year. This
would include the specific and usually incremental changes necessary to
shift from what is currently being done to what is desired. Targets for
improved efficiency as well as service delivery are also established, so that
progress can be measured periodically. The major point is that the changes
must be made at this stage (if not before) to implement what has in effect
been promised in step 7.

STEP 9: PERIODIC EVALUATION OF SERVICES OFFERED AND
DOCUMENTATION OF CHANGING NEEDS

> TECHNIQUE:
> A. *Repetition of Steps 2 through 4.*
> B. *Preparation of Appropriate Reports and Resource Requests
>   Utilizing These Data for Justification*
> C. *Implementation of Changes in Technical Operations Where
>   Performance Inadequacies have been Identified in the Analysis
>   of the Data Collected*

Periodic review is essential not only to accommodate changing needs of clients but also to identify performance problems in implementing the services agreed to by the clients and the media staff. Continuous evaluation of the efficiency and effectiveness of all aspects of the program is also a necessity, as well as data collection to document achievement and justify requests for resources.

The process that has been outlined here and that will be discussed in detail in later chapters attempts to provide the process and tools necessary for a media staff to plan and develop responsive programs more systematically and rationally, to communicate more effectively, and to provide more adequate documentation of what is done, why it is done, and what resources are required to do it. This process, however, can be threatening to some individuals. When clients participate in deciding program offerings and clearly understand what they have a right to expect, they are in a better position to judge whether what was promised is delivered. This, then, provides a concrete basis for media program accountability to clients.

The implementation of these planning procedures also requires time, and many people feel that this takes too much time away from actually doing. There are many rationalizations for not expending time and energy on systematic program planning. However, if we are going to justify and make the best use of resources in order to provide the maximum and most appropriate services possible in a given situation, is there any alternative? Can we accurately and comprehensively intuit client needs and appropriate program responses, and also document the validity of these intuitions with the precision and detail required by accountability-conscious administrators and boards?

CHAPTER 3

Definition of
Program Alternatives

A conceptually sound and coherent definition of program alternatives is basic to any planning activity. The basic framework or model and rationale for such a definition, as well as a brief history of the development of the instrument intended to be used for this purpose, was discussed in the previous sections. The "Inventory of School Library/Media Center Services" attempts to provide this definition and, therefore, the basic organization and structure for the other three planning instruments and planning techniques.

The basic concepts and considerations that are inherent in the design of this instrument or definition of media program alternatives can be summarized as follows:

1. The media program is viewed as an aggregation of services established to facilitate clients' learning and instructional goals and objectives. The "Inventory of School Library/Media Center Services" attempts to systematically delineate, as exhaustively as possible, the entire range of these potential or alternative services.

2. Services are expressed in terms of functions performed from the users' viewpoint in order to distinguish the "ends" of the media program from the "means" of the program. Also, some indication of the conditions under which the services are provided are included, where possible, to reflect user cost-benefit considerations such as the users' effort, time, and expense in utilizing the services.

   The strong emphasis on making means/ends distinctions is an extremely important conceptual element in the approach taken here and represents a serious attempt to move away from techniques for describing and evaluating media programs on the basis of quantities of resources alone. Quantities of resources—whether they reflect size of collection, number of books per pupil, number of nonprint items per pupil, or number of staff per pupil—are *means* and do not describe specific services offered to users. The approach reflected in the "Inventory of School Library/Media Center Services" is meant to lead beyond the simple description of what media centers *have* to what media programs can actually *do* for users.

3. The exhaustive list of services is clustered into five major categories, each with a number of subcategories. This approach was taken to simplify use and clarify functions, as well as to facilitate the identification and analysis in later steps of the resource and operational requirements of each service. Considerable experimentation was performed with different categorizations, but the resulting five tended to be meaningful to most media specialists and achieve the discriminations necessary in the other planning steps. The objective was to define each category and each service in such a way as to be as discrete as possible and not overlap or duplicate any other—recognizing, of course, that all of these services are closely related. This is very difficult to achieve since many different interpretations are always possible and no consensus regarding the uniform meaning and use of terminology has been developed in this field. The distinctions made in the "Inventory of School Library/Media Center Services" and other instruments, however, have been thoroughly tested and are workable, though some initial familiarization is necessary. The distinctions are certainly not absolute or perfect, and in a number of cases are arbitrary, but it is necessary to begin to view and describe media programs and services consistently if effective planning and communication is to be achieved.

Within each of the five discrete kinds or categories of service the subarrangement attempts to be hierarchical, moving from "least" to "most" service in user terms or from the least complex or difficult to the most complex services. An example of this continuum, illustrated in figure 5, would be the simple provision of reference materials for self-help, at one extreme, and the complete performance of the service, in terms of providing answers to questions, at the other end. It is obvious that the more one approaches staff performance of a

| SELF-HELP | STAFF | STAFF PERFORMS |
| COLLECTION | ASSISTANCE | SERVICE (ANSWERS) |

Fɪɢ. 5. Service continuum

service for users or the more complex services, the greater the resources needed to support the media program. This approach therefore provides a clear reflection of levels of service, but in terms that have distinct resource and operational implications.

4. The services are expressed "behaviorally" as much as possible, in terms of what is actually done for or provided to the user rather than in terms of the ultimate intent of providing the service. The intent and value of each service can therefore be judged locally and the services can be expressed much more explicitly.

5. The "Inventory of School Library/Media Center Services" is intended for elementary (excluding student use), middle or junior, and secondary programs and has been tested at these levels. Modifications suggested by some for elementary programs were felt to be too slight to sacrifice consistency and were frequently more of a reflection of the limitations of local circumstances than a valid judgment of the viability at least potentially of some of the services for elementary programs. The instrument is not intended to portray a simplistic or constrictive view of media programs or service alternatives since this is felt to be counterproductive in the long range.

6. As explained in chapter 2, the "Inventory of School Library/Media Center Services" is constructed in the form of a survey instrument, to be used in step 2 of the planning process, but also because this was felt to be an effective form of presenting the service alternatives to clients and media staff. The "Inventory" also serves as the glossary of fullest definition for the other instruments, which are structured and categorized according to the services defined in this instrument and explained in this chapter. Some local interpretations will inevitably be necessary, but as long as they are uniformly understood and applied, this should not create a serious problem in the use of the instruments.

Major Categories of Service

The five major kinds or categories of service are:

"*I. Access to Materials, Equipment, and Space.*" This basic service category includes the provision of collections of print and nonprint materials, equipment, and the space to use these items, as well as other media-related activities. Also included is the provision of materials and equipment external to the school by means of loan or network arrangements. This service category is listed first not because it is the most traditional service category or the most important but because it is fundamental or at least supportive of many of the other services.

"*II. Reference Services.*" The information-providing function or activities (versus materials or equipment) are included in this category. Information is extracted or obtained from various sources in relation to a specific request or perceived need, compared to simply providing previously packaged information—for example, books in "I. Access to Materials, Equipment, and Space." Providing information through various current awareness and bibliographic activities is included, as well as reference tools for self-help, reference assistance, and question-answer services.

"*III. Production Services.*" The provision of the materials, equipment, and facilities for producing new or adapted materials with various methods is included here, in addition to technical assistance and the actual production of materials or products for clients by the media staff.

"*IV. Instruction.*" Formal and informal instructional activities, as well as in-service and reading, viewing, and listening guidance activities, are included in this category. The orientation of these activities is to "familiarize" clients—to develop, for example, reading interests and skills or to extend client independence in the utilization of media resources and equipment.

"*V. Consulting Services.*" Consultation only for teachers and school staff is included here, with student consultation placed under either "Reference" or "Instruction," depending on the activity. Consulting in terms of selection and use of instructional resources is included, as well as assistance in instructional planning for individuals and teams and participation at the departmental or grade level and school and district level.

Service Subcategories

Each major service category is subdivided, where possible, according to the hierarchical considerations described previously, and where this is not possible according to considerations of user convenience and the relative costs of providing the services. A serious attempt was made to define each service subcategory as a discrete item, but obviously some ambiguities and varying interpretations are not only possible but inevitable. Generally accepted terms are used where possible, but where common terminology is ambiguous or misleading, other terms are substituted; and some illustrations and elaborations are given, although these were kept to a minimum to prevent the planning instrument from becoming too long and cumbersome. The major areas of confusion are discussed below.

"I. ACCESS TO MATERIALS, EQUIPMENT, AND SPACE"

"*A. Provision of Materials.*" The major kinds of software provided either through direct access (for example, open shelves) or through restricted access (which requires the client to ask for the items) are itemized here. The intent is to reflect at least the range of materials to which access is provided by an in-center collection, and the later instruments include more extensive quantitative descriptions of the collection. The terms attempt to provide an extensive description of the major kinds of materials but not necessarily an exhaustive list.

"*B. Provision of AV Equipment.*" The major categories of equipment that are made available for client use are listed and the same considerations apply as in "I. Access to Materials, Equipment, and Space; A. Provision of Materials." Equipment which should be excluded here and placed under "III. Production Services" is equipment which is solely or almost entirely used for production functions described under that category. However, this kind of problem of where a certain piece of equipment or other item fits when it has a multiple service function usually arises only in data collection and cost analysis, which is explained in greater detail in later chapters.

The only major confusion with terminology in this section usually occurs with the "automated learning and information retrieval systems." This is intended simply as a general term, incorporating all the newer and more sophisticated approaches developed in information systems for individualized learning. A few examples are given, but here—particularly—whatever systems are available in a local situation should be added. Here also, as in many places in the "Inventory of School Library/Media Center Services," distinctions regarding the availability of services by client group—namely, teachers and students—must also be made explicit.

"*C. Provision of Space*" and "*D. Use of Materials, Equipment, and Space.*" These two subcategories are seen as supporting the previous service subcategories in this major category, as well as some other services, and particularly in the case of "I. Access to Materials, Equipment, and Space; C. Provision of Space." The kinds of space for individual and group use which are provided, as well as a detailed description of the conditions under which materials, equipment, and space may be used by clients, are included in these two subcategories. The conditions under which these services are made available obviously constitute a very significant factor from the clients' viewpoint. This is one reason why a separate subcategory was established in this category of service—as well as to eliminate the need for duplicating these extensive use conditions in several places. The conditions under which services are provided for subcategories other than A through C, however, are normally included in each service subcategory.

"*E. Provision of Materials Not in the Media Center Collection.*" The various levels of service regarding the obtaining of materials from other sources, for example, borrowing from other media centers or libraries are included here as well as the selling of materials to users and acquiring special materials on request. The provision of information regarding materials located outside the center's collection versus actually borrowing the materials is however included under "II. Reference Services, C. Identification and Location of Materials Not in the Media Center."

"*F. Special Collections.*" The provision of special collections in the center or to classrooms is included. This would include reserve collections, small collections on a specific subject related to an instructional unit collected and placed for a period of time in a classroom, and more extensive special collections such as a professional library for teachers.

"*G. Copying.*" The provision of simple copying facilities for users and the conditions of use are included here since the function served is related to making the use of materials more convenient and thus extends the access provided to materials. The more elaborate kinds of copying involving, for example, audio recording and photographic processes are included as is common with "III. Production Services, A. Provision of Materials," although a case could be made to include some of this as simple copying of already-produced materials under this service category.

"II. REFERENCE SERVICES"

"*A. Provision of Reference Materials for Self-Help.*" The most basic level of service includes, simply, the provision of reference sources for client use. Obviously, many more sources are commonly used to fulfill this function than those that are clearly identified as reference tools. However, in most cases the tools that are specifically and/or primarily designed for this function can be identified, and reference use can be discriminated from other kinds of use. This distinction also becomes very useful in analysis of costs of services since the cost differential of these resources, compared to many other materials in "I. Access to Materials, Equipment, and Space; A. Provision of Materials," is significant.

"*B. Identification and Location of Materials in the Media Center.*" In this subcategory "assistance" is defined rather narrowly to include only assistance in identifying and locating materials—not provision of information or answers, as in later subcategories of "II. Reference Services." This, the lowest level of reference assistance, still keeps the burden of the inquiry on the client, with the media specialist simply helping the client resolve rather simple bibliographic identification or locational problems.

A frequent problem occurs here because of the natural inclination not only to provide assistance but to include an instructional sermonette, thus raising the question of whether what one is doing is reference or informal instruction. The difference can be very subtle, but in most cases the discrimination can be made. These approaches are quite different, on the one hand providing specific assistance when a need arises and, on the other hand, providing instruction with the objective of making the user self-sufficient. The position taken here is that these are distinctly different services with different objectives and implications for the user.

Making the distinction between reference assistance on demand and instruction also permits the seemingly endless debate about the efficacy of the different approaches to be resolved at the local level on the basis of the philosophy, objectives, and values of those involved. It also facilitates the measurement and evaluation of the efficiency and effectiveness of these two approaches in facilitating a user's interaction with information resources.

"*C. Identification and Location of Materials Not in the Media Center.*" Providing information about resources available for use but external to the school, making arrangements on request for clients to use these resources, and maintaining files of information on other libraries and information resources are to be considered part of this service.

"*D. Alerting the User and Current Awareness Services.*" These activities are normally provided in anticipation of a client need and are intended to increase the awareness and use of services, materials, and so forth by clients. Some of these activities are frequently referred to as public relations activities. Information regarding new acquisitions and services, special programs and publicity, and personal presentations, as well as systematic efforts at assessing and recording client needs and interests, are included in this subcategory.

"*E. Assistance in Compiling Bibliographies.*" Bibliographic assistance in the "Inventory of School Library/Media Center Services" ranges from provision of assistance to a client in compiling a list of references to conducting extensive searches and evaluations of the materials identified on demand or in anticipation of demand. Also included are arrangements provided for client access to various searching services, for example, the Educational Resources Information Center (ERIC).

"*F. Answer Services.*" In this service a major responsibility for obtaining the information to respond to questions varying from simple to complex is accepted by the media specialist. This service is in sharp contrast to simply helping clients find information or instructing them so that they can help themselves. This includes the use of subject matter specialists at the highest level of service. The effort is to make explicit the distinctions among alternative services or approaches varying from the furnishing of information on request ("II. Reference Services; F. Answer Services") to providing assistance in finding information on request ("II. Reference Services; B. Identification and Location of Materials in the Media Center") to providing instruction to make it possible for clients to help themselves ("IV. Instruction").

"III. PRODUCTION SERVICES"

"*A. Provision of Materials for Use by Students and/or Teachers*"; "*B. Provision of Assistance in Production*"; "*C. Production of Materials by Media Center Staff for Users.*" The progression of services in this major service category is very similar to the progression in "II. Reference Services." The lowest level, A, is simply the provision of the basic materials, equipment, and space for users to produce or adapt materials. The next level, B, also provides technical assistance to users in performing the various categories of production functions, namely, graphics, reprography, and photography. The third level, C, not only involves the staff's producing materials for clients but usually more elaborate and complex productions requiring greater technical expertise, as well as more sophisticated equipment and materials. Television production and distribution is also included because some building-level programs perform some of these functions, although the most common pattern is for these functions to be provided from the district or regional level.

"IV. INSTRUCTION"

"*A. Directional Services.*" The first level of instructional services is simply the provision of information about the media center and its services in a variety of forms. The intent is basically to provide information to permit the client to help himself.

"*B. Formal Instruction and Orientation Programs.*" Formal instructional services involve scheduled and structured activities, usually on a group basis, and examples of areas or kinds of instruction are listed. Formal instruction is categorized as a lower-level service than informal instruction because it is less responsive to user convenience; for example, it is scheduled, versus available on demand, and, is provided to groups rather than on an individual basis or individually tailored.

"*C. In-Service Training.*" Whereas subcategories B, D, and E focus on instructional services to students, this subcategory focuses on instructional activities to teachers and other school staff. Again, as in subcategory B, a number of examples of areas of instruction are included.

"*D. Informal Instruction.*" This service stresses individual instruction on request and lists a number of illustrative areas or kinds of instruction. As indicated under "II. Reference Services; B. Identification and Location of Materials in the Media Center," informal instruction is intended to teach the users to be independent and involves calculated instructional strategies rather than simply providing assistance without instructional content or intent.

"*E. Guidance in Reading, Viewing, and Listening.*" A variety of activities is included under this subcategory, all with the objective of providing individual or group guidance, encouragement, and instruction toward improving reading, viewing, and listening skills and interest and appreciation. One specific kind of activity, which is not included in the elaboration of this service but which should definitely be included in this subcategory, is story telling.

"V. CONSULTING SERVICES"

"*A. Advising Individual Teachers*"; "*B. Advising Teaching Teams and Department or Grade-Level Groups*"; "*C. Overall Curriculum Planning.*" This service area includes media staff consultations with teachers individually (A), in teams and so forth (B), and with overall school curriculum committees or district-level curriculum committees (C). The content of the consultations can vary from selection and use of media and media services in teaching and use of professional or curricular materials to involvement and advising on the design of instructional strategies and content. The latter goes far beyond traditional consulting activities and closely involves the media specialist in systematic instructional planning and development, and therefore requires the expertise necessary to provide this level of consultative assistance and direction.

"*D. Media Clearinghouse.*" The term "clearinghouse" is used to emphasize the intermediary nature of this very specific information and materials dissemination. The materials of concern are those instructional materials or resources which are not and will not normally become a part of the media center collection and are usually purchased with other than media program funds. These resources will be located and used in classrooms and departments, but samples or various kinds of evaluative information are provided by the media staff to facilitate the selection of these resources by the teaching staff. This service occurs in conjunction with curricular planning by individual teachers or curricular planning groups, which explains the placement of this subcategory at the end of this service category.

The major service categories and subcategories are also discussed in later chapters in relation to collecting program data and program analysis. This additional description and interpretation of services should also be consulted for clarification of the content and structure of the "Inventory of School Library/Media Center Services."

NOTE

1. Before one reads this discussion of the service subcategories, a review of "Inventory of School Library/Media Center Services" (appendix A) would be beneficial. All roman numeral and capital letter references refer to service categories or subcategories in the "Inventory."

CHAPTER 4

Assessing Service Needs
and Priorities

The "what" and the "why" of the two techniques or instruments for measuring perceptions of services, the "Inventory of School Library/Media Center Services," and for determining service needs and priorities, the "Form for Determining Preferences for School Library/Media Center Services," were discussed under steps 2 and 3 of the planning process in chapter 2. The present chapter treats in greater detail the "how"—or the procedures employed in using these techniques and executing these two planning steps.

Service Awareness Survey

Use of the "Inventory of School Library/Media Center Services" as a self-administered questionnaire in a survey of client and staff perceptions or awareness of media services, as recommended in step 2 of the planning process, is the first step in performing a more systematic, objective, and broadly based needs assessment. In this way the first need measured is for awareness or knowledge of the meaning and utility of media services, as well as the conditions of their availability. The "Inventory of School Library/Media Center Services" is designed not only to capture information regarding client as well as staff awareness (or lack of awareness), it also, because of the comprehensive and user output–oriented description of services, serves as the initial vehicle for communicating services and beginning the clarification of misconceptions or lack of awareness of services. The education of clients and staff regarding alternative or potential, as well as currently available, media services is critical if effective and participative needs assessment as well as proper use is to occur.

Implicit in this approach is the conviction that client involvement in assessing needs and determining priorities is not only desirable but essential in accomplishing a responsive and effective service program founded on a valid diagnosis of needs and use preferences.

INITIAL STEPS

Authorization and support by the appropriate administrative official, usually the school principal—as well as the willing cooperation of the clients who will participate in the survey—must be procured if the objectives of the survey are to be achieved. The most common procedure is to present the objectives and plan for the implementation of the entire planning process to the principal and teachers very early in the initial planning phase, as is detailed in chapter 7. This approval and support is particularly necessary for steps 2 and 3 of the planning process since the time not only of the media staff but also of the teachers, students, and administrative staff is involved. In the experience of the writer, administrators, teachers, and students are very responsive and cooperative if the objectives of assessing needs and developing more responsive and effective services are clearly presented, since it is very apparently in their self-interest. Administrators have been particularly responsive, probably because they are more sensitive to accountability pressures as well as more familiar with the newer systematic planning techniques.

A warning is prudent against the very unwise tactic of distributing survey instruments to individuals without prior explanation. A personal presentation in a general meeting (for example, a teachers' meeting) is usually much more effective in eliciting a receptive reaction—and also in achieving more serious responses—than simply distributing the instruments, to be returned at some later date. An expression of the support of the administration for the survey and its objectives is also extremely helpful at this time.

SELECTION OF PARTICIPANTS

Because increasing client awareness of media services is the primary objective and assessing awareness gaps and areas of ineffectiveness of media program communication is secondary, the ideal is to include everyone in the survey. Conducting a survey on this scale, it should also be noted, achieves greater visibility for the media program. This is frequently not possible, however—particularly with a large student population. In such a case a sampling approach is suggested for the survey in order to minimize the time required, expense, and logistical problems. Nonetheless, even where only a sampling approach seems feasible, a few possibilities should be considered:

Teachers. Include all teachers rather than a representative sample. Even in a large school, the number of teachers is small enough to handle. Teachers play the central role in planning and directing the instructional activities which are the primary stimuli or generators of student information and service needs and use. Therefore, to maximize the media program's effectiveness with students as well as with teachers it would seem advisable to be as inclusive as possible when considering what proportion of teachers to include in both step 2 and step 3 of the planning process.

Students. Include all students—or as many as possible—but in order to reduce the tabulation time and problems, analyze only a 10 to 20 percent representative sample of those survey instruments completed. The initial exposure to a comprehensive and user-oriented description of media services (the educational objective) can be achieved with the survey, even without tabulating and analyzing all of the filled-out instruments. Analysis of a representative sample of the returns will just as reliably identify awareness and communication problems, the secondary objective, without decreasing the number of students involved in attempting to achieve the primary objective.

Sample of the student population. If only a sample of the student population is to be surveyed,

First, systematically select a 10 percent sample of the students. The factors which should be considered in determining sample size, as well as selecting individuals for the sample, are the desired reliability, the user-group population size, the number of significant user-group characteristics, the heterogeneity of the user group, and the time and money available for conducting the survey. To achieve a representative sample which reflects the differences in the total population, it may be desirable to increase the size of the sample if one or more factors (other than population size) are extremely high or large.

Second, select a method which will ensure adequate representation. Regardless of the size of the sample, the method of selecting the individuals is extremely important to ensure adequate representation. Subjective selections (on whatever basis) by the media staff or teachers should be avoided so as not to introduce either known or unknown biases into the selection of the sample.

Obtain a list of all students in the total population. If the population is 500 and the sample size, therefore, is 50, one can select every tenth name (for example, the 10th, 20th, 30th, and so on) until all fifty are selected. However, one does not have to start in such an orderly fashion, in that one could select the 3d, 13th, 23d, and so on by randomly choosing the starting point.[1]

LOGISTICS

Some of the arrangements and details of administering a survey of this kind can be problematical. The "Inventory of School Library/Media Center Services" was developed as a self-administered survey instrument— and blanket permission for duplication for surveys of the kind under discussion is granted. However, it may be advantageous (for a number of reasons, for example, paper costs and ease of tabulation) to construct a simple answer sheet for the responses and then duplicate only enough copies of the instrument to accommodate the largest group to which it is administered. If this is done, numbers or an identifying designation will probably have to be assigned to each possible response (rather than to each question, as is done on the form) on the "Inventory of School Library/Media Center Services" to correspond with the numbers on the answer sheet. Also, the response boxes or format on the instrument will have to be replicated on the answer sheet to accommodate the various responses. (See appendix F for a suggested format.) This approach is also advantageous if one plans to assess awareness of media services periodically, for example, with new students and staff, since the sample instruments can be used repeatedly. However, an answer sheet places an additional burden on the respondent and therefore is not the most desirable approach (unless it is necessary for the reasons mentioned).

It is strongly recommended that administration of the survey, particularly to students, be done with groups under the supervision of the media staff or individuals who are very familiar with the questionnaire. If this approach is used, an initial explanation can be given of the purposes of the survey, and instructions and assistance can be given where warranted. Most can complete the survey in approximately thirty minutes. The survey is usually taken more seriously if it is handled in this manner, and those who have reading problems can be identified so that assistance can be given. Those with serious reading problems should be identified and, rather than be eliminated from the survey, should be handled separately —if possible, by reading the questionnaire to them and recording the responses. In giving the initial explanation, as well as responding to questions, the individual who administers the survey should be warned not to give too much explanation regarding the media services, or the results of the survey will be invalid.

It should be stressed that it is the perceptions of the media services that are offered, regardless of how inaccurate these perceptions may be, that are being sought. Consequently, there are no right or wrong answers, and it is as inappropriate to ask the media staff if it provides a service as for the media staff to explain in such detail that the perceptions of the respondents are influenced. The correction or clarification of misperceptions is done later, when the results of the survey are reported, or through follow-up instructional activities.

TABULATION OF RESULTS

Counting the responses and recording them on a master form or copy of the instrument is a simple but time-consuming task, and is frequently done by students, volunteers, or aides. The analysis can be done many ways, but it is common to compute (separately) the percent of teachers and students who responded to each question positively or negatively. These percentages are then compared to the responses of the media staff to identify areas and degrees of agreement and disagreement. This analysis can show how effectively service policies have been communicated, areas of confusion among groups in need of clarification, service inconsistencies, and conflicting staff implementations of policies. Charts or tables can then be constructed to show major and (if desired) minor misconceptions of services offered by students and/or teachers. This can also be done with areas where services are well understood. If teachers have been identified by department or grade level and students by grade level, a further analysis can be done to reveal if there are awareness problems with particular groups of individuals. This is particularly useful in planning and structuring instructional activities that are targeted at identified problems with specific groups of individuals.

The media staff should also complete the "Inventory of School Library/ Media Center Services" as a preliminary activity and then compare the results, since it is very common to find almost as many variations in responses among staff members in some areas as between the reponses of media staff and clients. The discrepancies should then be reconsidered so that agreement is achieved for purposes of comparison with the responses of teachers, students, and administrators. A usual by-product is a much more consistent interpretation of service policies by the media staff. This can provide the basis for a more extensive and publicized service policy that covers *all* service areas, not only those that are traditionally covered (such as circulation policies). In a number of cases this approach, as well as use of the "Form for Determining Preferences for School Library/Media Center Services," has been used as in-service training for the media staff.

This technique can also be used as a periodic measurement of the effectiveness of the instructional, orientation, and communication programs of the media center, at least in terms of service awareness. Continued use of the technique in orienting new students and teachers is also possible. This provides an opportunity for following up with the assessment of needs and service values to maintain a current and comprehensive picture of the needs and preferences of the entire client group, including those who are new to the school.

COMMUNICATION

The results of the survey should be communicated back to all client groups through (for example) formal presentations, newspaper articles, or a widely distributed report. This becomes the second step in the education process (which began with the survey) and is an excellent opportunity for a wide variety of follow-up instructional activities directed at identified problems.

Determining Service Needs and Priorities

The decisions regarding which services will be provided, to whom, and under what conditions are possibly the most critical decisions made by the media staff, at least from the clients' viewpoint. The objective in step 3 of the planning process is to carefully determine the service priorities or the relative importance or desirability of various alternative media-service arrangements for a specific school or group of clients. The process attempts to consider such things as local instructional goals and objectives, varying instructional strategies, and special client needs. The strategy for accomplishing this needs assessment is to provide a process in which the clients themselves express and interpret their goals, objectives, needs, and values while participating with the media staff in systematically determining the media-service priorities for their school.

In the development and testing of this process, the surprising power of this technique to generate vigorous and broad involvement, intense interest, and vastly expanded awareness was very encouraging. This tends to provide considerable encouragement and reinforcement for the media staff, as well as a pleasurable and enlightening experience for the clients. This kind of reaction is frequently unanticipated, however, by most individuals and frequently leads to requests for more time in the group sessions to pursue the process in more depth. This would seem to be a positive and encouraging sign, but in the writer's experience no one seems to be willing to expect such positive reactions, even when "warned," until they actually occur.

The procedures or sequence of activities in this service-priority determination technique can be expressed in the following series of substeps.

SUBSTEP 1

It is assumed that the initial explanation of the objectives and procedures involving client participation have been accomplished and approval given for the use of the client time that is necessary at this stage. If a planning advisory committee has not been established by this time, involving teachers, administrators, students, and media staff, it would be useful to do so at this juncture. The logistical decisions on who is involved in the process and the scheduling of the group meetings are important and potentially problematical. Participation of a representative group in making these decisions can alleviate or minimize a number of these problems. Close involvement of the appropriate administrator is particularly necessary at this stage.

An estimate of the approximate time needed for various activities is as follows:

Initial explanation to teachers at a faculty meeting—15–30 minutes

Individual completion of the "Form for Determining Preferences for School Library/Media Center Services"—30 minutes

First group meeting—2 to 3 hours, or somewhat longer if it is split into smaller units and spread over a period of time

Follow-up group meeting—1 hour

It is highly desirable to arrange the first group meeting in one block of time. The total time necessary is reduced if this is possible and momentum toward consensus is not deflated prior to achieving agreement. In-service days, after-school hours, and substitutes have all been used to enable individuals to participate in group sessions. The local school situation and the degree of administrative support will undoubtedly influence or even determine the scheduling of the group sessions.

SUBSTEP 2

Selection of a representative group of students (middle school and above), teachers, and administrative staff must be made of those who have participated in step 2 of the planning process. These individuals are asked to be the representatives and to participate with the media staff in the process which will determine the media service preferences and priorities for the school. There are no absolute criteria for the makeup of this representative group; however, some of the factors which should be considered in order to reflect adequately the variety of needs and values represented in the school are the various subject departments or grade levels in the school program, the different instructional strategies or teaching styles, non-use—as well as use—of present services, and student achievement, interests, cultural background, and career goals. Judgment should be exercised in selecting the sample, and willingness to cooperate—as well as the need to incorporate "influentials" or individuals of high "visibility," political influence, and authority—are legitimate considerations. These latter considerations are particularly relevant in order to maximize the dissemination and acceptance of the ideas and the increased awareness developed in the priority determination process. The use of established groups or organizations (for example, a student council) may be particularly helpful in achieving good representation as well as the "semblance" of good representation.

The size of the group is important, and should not exceed twenty, but the probable ideal size is around ten. The process requires, and generates, intense interaction, which is necessary if preferences and values are to be freely expressed and reasonable agreement eventually achieved. This kind of interaction cannot occur as well as it needs to if the group is too large. Frequently, to reduce group size and achieve greater representation, several separate groups (such as grade-level or department groups and a separate student group) are selected to carry out the priority determination process separately (substeps 3 and 4) and then representatives are selected from each group to comprise the final group for determining the overall priorities. This approach has a number of advantages: it enables greater participation of individuals in department or grade-level or student groups; it provides specific data on need and preference variations among these different groups; it enables the formation of groups small enough to be effective; and it provides the student representatives initial training and confidence building so as to minimize the possibility that they will be intimidated by faculty or administrators in the give and take of the overall group session. Participation is not usually difficult to get; however, if natural interest and willingness to help must be supplemented, the opportunity to represent needs and influence the services provided can be stressed as incentives.

SUBSTEP 3

The individuals who are selected to participate are given copies of the "Form for Determining Preferences for School Library/Media Center Services" and the "Inventory of School Library/Media Center Services." They are asked to complete the former prior to the scheduled group session and to consult the latter for further explanation of the preference form, since it is simply an abbreviated version in outline form. The participants are asked to follow the instructions that accompany the form and, if possible, report their responses to the media specialist so that all individual responses can be recorded on a large master display in preparation for the group session.

The procedure (explained in the instructions) requires the respondent to allocate an arbitrary number of points (in this case 1,000) among the entire range of potential service alternatives. The distribution of points should precisely reflect the relative value of these alternative services in meeting their individual needs. The individuals should consider the educational goals, objectives, the instructional or learning strategies with which they are involved and the resultant service needs and use preferences.

The arbitrary number of points is necessary in order to force careful choices and discriminations among alternatives in a situation analogous to the real world, where there are practical limitations and not everything is possible. However, respondents should be urged to assign values only on the basis of need and preference, regardless of what is currently offered or what seems feasible. What may appear to be unfeasible or impractical at the moment may become possible if enough support is generated and the need is demonstrated. It is important to get a clear expression of what is needed and valued at this point, and the feasibility factors should be considered later (in step 6 of the planning process, at which point the discrepancy between need and capability can be clearly identified and used as documentation to justify resource requests).

SUBSTEP 4

The next step is to hold the group consensus-building session and the preliminary group sessions, if the two-step approach is used. The objective is amalgamation of individual service preferences into one statement of priorities that represents the optimal arrangement of service offerings which can best serve the needs of the total client population. Individual preferences of each participant in the major categories and subcategories should be displayed so that the entire group can easily see them during the discussion. This can be accomplished by recording (on newsprint or a chalkboard) the outline of the "Form for Determining Preferences for School Library/Media Center Services," with one-word reminders down the left-hand column, and constructing enough columns to record the values of each participant (plus an extra column for recording the consensus figures as they are worked out).

The manner in which the group session is conducted is important, and it should establish a spirit of reasonableness and cooperation (not everything can be done and everyone cannot insist on his preferences, because everyone has a right to service). The leadership skills of the group leader are important, and where the media specialist feels inadequate another individual can perform this role, with the media specialist acting as a resource for interpretation and explanation. Social pressures, the dynamics of the group, and political ability all contribute to achieving agreement. Student participation is usually quite active and provides a healthy influence on the other participants, in addition to helping maintain a student-oriented focus. The media specialist should play an active role in explaining, interpreting, and pointing out the advantages and disadvantages of various approaches, but he—or she—should not dominate the group so as to distort or stifle the expression of client needs and values. The media specialist should assert professional expertise and judgment by developing understanding, rather than by authoritarian pronouncements, if a collegial and participative relationship is to be effective.

The process employed in conducting the session is identical to that followed by the individuals initially in completing the form, beginning with tentative agreement on the major service categories and proceeding to the subcategories. To begin the process, the high and the low values given to each service category and subcategory should be pointed out and the individuals who express those values should discuss their position. A considerable number of the initial differences will be due to a lack of understanding of the services or the process, and therefore considerable time should be devoted at the beginning to explanation and interpretation, without pressing too rapidly for agreement. Exchanges between the participants in explaining their activities and needs are useful for increasing mutual understanding and awareness. However, after a common understanding of the terms and services is developed, real value and need differences will be expressed, and they should be handled through negotiation and accommodation. There must be some give and take, some tradeoffs. Group pressure will usually overcome particularly stubborn views, but if not, irreconcilable differences can be dealt with by averaging the conflicting values or selecting some number of points between the extremes with which the majority agree. Extreme or unique service values should be recorded if the justification seems reasonable or a unique situation is identified that warrants special consideration. Consideration can be given at a later time to tailoring services (at least in unusual cases) to particular situations to the degree that available resources permit, without dishonoring or distorting the priorities agreed upon.

Some common problems or issues, which frequently occur and which should be anticipated, are as follows.

Assigning values. Resistance is occasionally expressed to the use of quantities, 1,000 points, to express values. Assigning values is difficult, and this system may initially seem artificial, but it works well in terms of reflecting client needs and preferences—in a valid and reasonably precise way and in a fashion which can readily be translated into service responses. In the writer's experience, most participants—in spite of initial misgivings but after experience with the process—agree that the technique is very powerful and useful and achieves its purpose in a reasonable manner. This kind of reassurance and solicitation of cooperation can normally overcome the initial resistance.

Ranking or weighting the services. The suggestion may be raised simply to rank the services according to value rather than weight them by using a point system. This is frequently a useful technique to start the consensus-building process but it is not discriminatory enough in terms of reflecting degrees of difference in value between services and does not provide the kind of specific distinctions necessary to make detailed program decisions.

For example, ranking three services in one service category in one–two–three order of importance gives some indication of relative value but not much, and it can even distort the picture. If, for example, 500 points out of 2,000 were allocated to this overall category and 400 of those points were placed on the first-ranked service, 95 on the second, and 5 on the third, a much different picture is presented than if a simple ranking is used. Obviously, the category is considered very important if 50 percent of the total value is placed on it, but the first-ranked service is of *utmost* importance—considerably more important than the second—and the third-ranked service is almost insignificant.

These kinds of discriminations are necessary for planning purposes and are not provided by a ranking system.

Distribution of points. A normal inclination, when one is first confronted with this valuing task, is to distribute the points—as much as possible—in order to get a "little bit of everything." This avoids making clear value distinctions, and would result in a terribly fractionated and ineffective program. It becomes clear, in doing a cost analysis of this kind of program, that a little bit of everything is a little bit of nothing for all but the few who are able to get a service when they need it. Encouragement should be given to *concentrate* points as much as possible on the highly valued areas so that the value or preference discriminations are clear and reasonably effective service responses can be developed.

The distribution of points will also inevitably reflect, at least to some degree, local conditions. For example, if the media program is new or has been historically and severely underfunded, the tendency seems to be to place more value on providing materials and equipment. If, however, a program has been reasonably well established, there seems to be a tendency to place more value on other services. This is very likely a reasonable position to take, but overconcern with feasibility should be avoided as much as possible for the reasons previously stated.

Instrument revision. Some instrument revision may be suggested and legitimately warranted. However, massive revision of the structure of the instrument may destroy its validity if the revisions are not made with a solid understanding of the principles upon which it was constructed. Some experience with the instrument is suggested before revisions should be considered.

Minimal numbers of points. A value of 5 or 10 points is minimal, and about the equivalent of zero, except in a few cases where demand may be small or a service may be possible with few resources. The distribution of small-number points should therefore be avoided, except in the above-mentioned cases or the arabic number or small-letter subdivisions of the service subcategories.

Agreement through discussion. Agreement should be achieved, if at all possible, through discussion rather than by averaging the values, because the resulting set of priorities would be grossly artificial and most of the constructive by-products of the process would be lost.

Tradeoffs. Tradeoffs among service categories and subcategories might be considered. For example, the relative emphasis placed on providing various reference assistance services on demand should be compared to the value placed on attempting to develop client self-sufficiency by stressing instructional services. These two services represent extremely different service positions and philosophies. Rather than being indecisive, perhaps it would be better to assign primary emphasis one way or the other in order to clearly establish and communicate the philosophy and primary thrust of the program. Another frequently debated issue is whether to emphasize "IV. Instruction; B. Formal Instruction" versus "IV. Instruction; D. Informal Instruction." At least, an expression of emphasis one way or another is more helpful in program planning than simply straddling the middle, which avoids decision.

Considerations of scale versus effectiveness also enter here, where, for example, one might take into account the value and effectiveness of reaching all or many students with large-group instruction versus not reaching as many but possibly being more effective with informal or individualized instruction and/or assistance.

Correlations between values and cost. There are apparent correlations between values and cost. However, at this stage the participants should think in terms of value as much as possible, without consideration of cost, since cost concerns may distort the accurate representation of needs and values.

SUBSTEP 5

The consensus on the relative value of the various services for the given situation is then reported back to the entire client population. This is done to test the validity of the relative values assigned by the smaller group and also to inform the clients of the priorities agreed upon. This can be done, for example, in teachers' meetings and the school newspaper, but feedback should be encouraged to determine if modifications need to be made to accommodate groups or significant needs which were overlooked. This also affords the media staff another opportunity for articulating the media program and its services. This reporting may also be combined effectively with reporting the results of the survey in step 2 of the planning process.

The priorities developed in this manner are recorded on the fourth instrument, described in chapter 6, in preparation for calculating program capability and program performance targets, as well as reallocations and additional resources that are necessary to achieve the agreed-upon priorities. Systematic and effective program planning and analysis cannot be accomplished without this kind of specific and measurable needs assessment and priority determination.

NOTE

1. These are simple suggestions which should provide reasonably accurate and useful data for the purpose intended but they do not represent the statistical procedures which would be used for research purposes. If greater reliability is desired, consult almost any introductory statistics textbook on the use of random sampling and random-number tables. Some useful suggestions, presented in a relatively simple fashion, can also be found in M. Carl Drott, "Random Sampling: A Tool for Library Research," *College and Research Libraries* 30:119–25 (March 1969). Also, some school districts have the capability of computer generation of a random list of students (for example, of any desired size for a given school) and the possibility of this service being available should be investigated.

CHAPTER 5

Program Planning Data

The application of systematic techniques to planning media programs requires many kinds of data and, in numerous causes, data which have not previously been collected. The kinds of data and the techniques discussed in chapters 5 and 6 are utilized to accomplish the remaining steps (4 to 9) in the planning process. Essentially, collection of these kinds of data, expressed in the manner suggested, enables one to accomplish—in a specific and documentable form—the following kinds of analyses.

1. Detailed comparisons of present service offerings and actual service outputs with the service needs and preferences of clients
2. Identification of the specific kinds and amounts of change required in the various service outputs in order to respond to client needs and preferences
3. Assessment of the resource and operational requirements and costs of present services, as well as the changes desired
4. Determination of which changes are possible and which are not in terms of resource, operational, and administrative constraints—for example, inability to reallocate funds from a materials budget category to a staff category in order to increase a service category primarily requiring staff time
5. Expression and documentation of specific implications for service outputs and the resulting responsiveness to client needs of potential or real increases or decreases in financial resources provided to the media program

Program Cost Accounting

The most basic and useful kind of data to be identified are specific cost data. However, cost in this context means more than simply the cost of basic resources; rather, it means total program costs in relation to delivering or achieving something—in this case a program of explicitly defined user services.

The primary concern in this approach is determination of the costs of operating ongoing media center programs, rather than the initial costs for establishing media center programs. To be able to determine the costs of specific service outputs it is necessary that the physical resources (for example, materials, equipment, and supplies) and operational means (the use of staff time to perform the necessary operations and procedures) required to provide a given service be precisely identified and translated into dollar costs. This obviously involves the application of cost accounting principles.

"Cost accounting" refers to procedures for determining the unit costs of products. As Mary E. Crookston explained in one of the earliest attempts to apply these procedures to school libraries, "Cost accounting is concerned with the determining of the costs of one activity or one unit of work."[1] The product in this case is a clearly defined user service, for which the units of resources and operational activities needed to provide the service must be determined and their costs estimated. The cost of a given service, provided at a specified level or scale of use, can be determined by totaling the costs of the requisite resource and operational units. Determining these discrete cost units for professional services is more difficult, and subject to many more variations, than for tangible products, but it is essential for systematic program planning.

Having defined the service outputs or products in the "Inventory of School Library/Media Center Services," we have the problem of identifying the requisite resource and operational units and determining the costing techniques and strategies. There are no standard or fully developed procedures for determining internal or operational costs of media programs. The approach here is to distinguish between direct and indirect costs, and to concentrate on direct costs since they are directly involved in operating the media center—and the media specialist has some control over them. The reasoning behind this approach is expressed in a report by Brutcher, Gessford, and Rixford: the cost of a unit of service output can be divided into direct costs (the materials and so forth and the labor employed to produce the output) and indirect costs (the overhead applicable to the output, such as depreciation of materials and buildings, utilities, and maintenance). The indirect costs usually are not closely associated with a given output.[2] Moreover, the media specialist has no control over indirect costs, because they are fixed. Thus it may legitimately be argued that budgetary planning would be more useful and much less complex if costs of outputs excluded overhead or indirect costs, since the media specialist could then perceive how he or she is controlling variable or direct costs.

The practice of dealing only with direct costs in order to stress a point of view or a particular objective is in line with standard procedures for the quantitative management of libraries or media programs. As Fred J. Heinritz states,

> In estimating costs, it is sometimes sensible to ignore overhead and/or depreciation and/or supply costs. However, they should not be omitted out of ignorance, for to do so is to delude oneself that the cost of an operation is less than it really is.[3]

Overhead and capital costs have therefore not been omitted out of ignorance but rather to facilitate the explanation and understanding of those resources *directly* involved in providing media center services. In overall long-range planning the need to consult and/or consider overhead and capital costs is clearly recognized (see appendix E).

Therefore, in this presentation, operating costs will be considered as *direct* costs and overhead and capital costs will be considered as *indirect* costs. The basic elements in each are:

DIRECT COSTS	INDIRECT COSTS
Labor (Staff Time)	*Overhead*
Materials	Administrative Services
Equipment	(School and District)
Supplies	Maintenance
	Utilities
	District Media Support Services
	Depreciation
	Capital
	Physical Facilities
	Initial Equipment
	Initial Collection

Some accounting procedures consider equipment as a capital cost, especially for major items such as television apparatus, but in this design equipment that is purchased out of the annual budget, after the initial equipping of the facility, is considered an operating cost. Moreover, many budgeting procedures treat supplies as overhead, but in this presentation supplies are treated as an operating cost because, like equipment, they can contribute directly and significantly to the provision of specific service outputs—for example, the production of materials.

To identify specific resource and operational units or elements in such a way as to relate them to specific service outputs, these direct cost elements are classified according to the model described in the first chapter (see also tables 1 and 2). These tables illustrate the process by which resources are acquired and converted, through the expenditure of staff time, into a program of user services. The basic formulas for deriving the costs of the resource and operational elements required to provide a specified service and program of services are as follows:

TABLE 1. MEDIA PROGRAM COSTING MODEL

INPUT ──────────────►	PROCESSING ──────────►	OUTPUT
Resource Costs	*Conversion or Operational Costs*	*Service Costs*
Materials	Application of Staff Time for	Specific User
Equipment	Technical Operations	Services at
Supplies	Management Operations	Given Use
Staff	Delivery Operations	Levels

Resource costs (materials, equipment, supplies). The number of units of each type of requisite resource, multiplied by the average unit cost of each type and added together, equals the estimated cost of resources for the specified service.

Conversion costs. The percent of (annual) time spent by staff members on the routines and operations related to a given service, multiplied by the appropriate salaries, equals the estimated operational or conversion cost of the specified service.

Output (service) cost. The resource and conversion costs are derived as explained above and are added together to determine the estimated total cost for providing each specified service.

Total program cost. The estimated total cost of providing the entire range of services in a given situation is derived by adding together the output (service) costs of each service offered.

Since the media center budget is allocated on a yearly basis, the costs of the program are likewise calculated on a yearly basis. Therefore resource costs refer to the yearly cost of providing the media center with materials, equipment, and supplies. The number of resource items refers to the quantity of a particular resource item (such as number of books, filmstrips, book jackets) purchased per year. The average unit cost of an item refers to the average cost of one particular resource item, derived from purchase

TABLE 2. REQUISITE RESOURCE AND CONVERSION COST FACTORS
   FOR SPECIFIED SERVICES

SERVICES =	RESOURCE COSTS			+ CONVERSION COSTS
	Materials	*Equipment*	*Supplies*	*Staff (Time)*
ACCESS TO MATERIALS, EQUIPMENT, AND SPACE	Yearly cost of collection development and replacement	Yearly cost of equipment additions and replacements	Yearly cost of supplies for processing, selection and evaluation circulation, and maintenance	Yearly cost of staff time for processing (acquisition and cataloging), selection and evaluation circulation, and maintenance of collection (inventory, etc.)
REFERENCE	Yearly cost of reference collection development and replacement			Yearly cost of staff time for reference
PRODUCTION	Yearly cost of materials for graphics, photography, reprography	Yearly cost of equipment additions and replacements	Yearly cost of supplies included with production materials	Yearly cost of staff time for production services and/or assistance
INSTRUCTION				Yearly cost of staff time
CONSULTA-TION				Yearly cost of staff time

invoices, catalogues, bidding lists, price lists, or simply by dividing the number of items purchased into the total amount expended. In some districts with centralized processing, this information, as well as other acquisition information, can be supplied by the district.

Conversion costs also refer to the yearly cost of media staff time spent on the operations necessary to provide a specified service. Operations have been categorized as technical operations (sometimes called technical services), referring to a *means* process in the overall production of service outputs, and delivery operations (sometimes called public service or user services), a *means* process referring to the activities involved in the delivery of a service to the user. The yearly cost of both operations is figured by identifying the technical and delivery operations or units, determining the average percent of yearly time of different staff members spent on these operations, and multiplying the yearly salary rate by the average percent of yearly time spent on the specific operation.

The total cost of a specific service is then derived simply by totaling all resource and time costs for that service. The total program cost is calculated similarly, by totaling the costs of all services offered. The accounting and mathematics are very simple; however, difficulty arises in collecting some kinds of data and in accounting for all the kinds and quantities of different items incorporated in operating media programs. In spite of their being relatively small-scale operations, media programs, upon examination, are very complex operations, which reinforces the need for using more systematic planning and managing techniques.

The "School Library/Media Program Data Collection Guide"

The "School Library/Media Program Data Collection Guide" (see appendix C) is designed to facilitate identifying and collecting the variety of program data required for systematic analysis, planning, managing, and reporting. Normally, a number of simple forms are developed by the local media staff to record the data as they are collected, since different individuals may be collecting them or different data may be collected at different times or in different ways. The forms are usually designed much like the "School Library/Media Program Data Collection Guide," but incorporate enough space or columns to record data for each sample incidence or day and for the total number of days sampled. Also, data which are readily available in records are not recorded since this would be a time-wasting duplication of effort. The singular objective here, however, is to use this guide (or locally developed forms) to collect the data required to complete the fourth instrument, the "School Library/Media Program Costing Matrix" (see appendix D and chapter 6).

The "School Library/Media Program Data Collection Guide," as well as the "School Library/Media Program Costing Matrix," are organized (left-hand columns) according to the service output categories of the "Inventory of School Library/Media Center Services," with appropriate *examples* of physical resources and staff operational or technical tasks listed with each service subcategory where these tasks are not clearly expressed in the wording of the service subcategory itself. Both the "School Library/Media Program Data Collection Guide" and the "School Library/Media Program Costing Matrix" have clarifying footnotes that should be read carefully.

The "School Library/Media Program Data Collection Guide" requires four categories of data in relation to each appropriate service category and subcategory:

1. Physical resources (subdivided into materials, equipment, and supplies) and costs
2. Staff time (translated into costs later in the "School Library/Media Program Costing Matrix")
3. Service outputs
4. Unfilled requests for service from users

The "School Library/Media Program Data Collection Guide" is divided into two parts, the first being "Physical Resources and Services Data" (see figure 6) and the second "Staff Time and Services Data" (see figure 7). The division into two parts is necessary to accommodate the different formats required to record these two kinds of data. Only those service subcategories that commonly require a significant and identifiable amount of physical resources are included in the first part. The only exclusion of service subcategories in part II is the provision of a reference collection ("II. Reference Services; A. Provision of Reference Materials for Self-Help") since the time spent on operational activities which should be recorded here is normally not distinguishable from the bulk of time spent on the similar activities which occur under provision of materials for all materials other than reference materials ("I. Access to Materials, Equipment, and Space; A. Provision of Materials").

PHYSICAL RESOURCES DATA

Quantities of resources. The current holdings (number of each type of item contained in the collection up to the current fiscal year), the number of items added, and the number of items replaced must be gathered from the media program records for each type of material and kind of equipment. The current-holdings information is included here for reference and as an indication of the current level of collection development. Since different items of information recorded in the "School Library/Media Program Costing Matrix" are later amalgamated for different analysis and reporting purposes, it is useful to have this significant information here, even though it is not used for cost or other calculations. Certain quantities (for example, periodicals and vertical file material) are problematical, but —however counted (for example, titles and volumes using two figures or numbers of folders in the case of the vertical file)—the method that is used should be applied consistently and defined in a footnote.

PHYSICAL RESOURCE ELEMENTS BY SERVICE SUBDIVISIONS	RESOURCE QUANTITIES				COSTS		SERVICE OUTPUTS		NUMBER OF UNFILLED REQUESTS
	CURRENT HOLDINGS	NUMBER ITEMS REPLACED	NUMBER ITEMS ADDED	TOTAL NO. ITEMS PURCHASED	COST RANGE	AVERAGE UNIT COST	In Center	Out of Center	

Fig. 6. Format of "Part I: Physical resources and services data"

SERVICE SUBDIVISIONS	OPERATIONAL TASKS	SAMPLE 1				SAMPLE 2, ETC.	DAILY AVERAGE	YEARLY AVERAGE
		TIME	SERVICE OUTPUTS	OPERATIONAL OUTPUTS	UNFILLED REQUESTS			

Fig. 7. Format of "Part II: Staff time and services data"

Even though this is not current practice generally, the number of items added and replaced should be identified separately so as not to reflect a grossly inflated picture of collection growth. The term "replacement" is not intended to indicate a title for title replacement but a professional judgment regarding the number of items which essentially replace out-dated, worn-out, or stolen items. This distinction can usually best be made when an item is selected and a record can be kept of the distinction, along with the normal acquisition records. The total number of items can then be calculated as the sum of the numbers of items added plus those replaced. This total number is also recorded.

Costs. The average unit cost for each item must be calculated, perhaps from a small random sample of costs of acquisitions or by simply dividing the amount expended for this item by the number purchased. The cost range—the cost of the most expensive acquisition minus the least expensive acquisition of a specific item—may also be calculated, where appropriate, to indicate the potential variation of the unit cost figures. Or simply the cost range for an item (highest and lowest figures) could be recorded.

Thus, for planning purposes, the full range of potential costs is known. The cautious planner might wish to use the higher end of the cost range, when determining needed resources, just to be sure to request sufficient financial support to accommodate inflation and so forth. This is particularly useful with expensive items, where the cost range is extreme and the items that are used to calculate an average cost are not characteristic and may (for example) reflect items only at the cheap end of the scale.

Supplies. The supplies can be handled in the same manner as materials and equipment, or by lumping them together into one or more appropriate service subcategories, but at least estimates of supply costs must be included. General supplies (paper, transparency sheets, folders, and so forth) are frequently difficult to break down by service output category. Moreover, there are so many different supplies that the "School Library/Media Program Data Collection Guide" lists only a few key examples, with space allotted for more if the staff wishes to add more supply categories. The number of supplies used and the average cost (for each category) can be recorded in the service categories where greatest usage occurs. The most common practice is to record all or most supply costs with provision of materials ("I. Access to Materials, Equipment, and Space; A. Provision of Materials") as a lump sum with a descriptive footnote.

It is important to discriminate as much as possible (within reason) and to record significant amounts of supply costs when they occur in the service subcategory to which they are related. Otherwise, the costs of the service subcategory charged will be distorted upward and the costs of the other subcategory artificially reduced. The "Production Services" category (III) is a good example where supply costs can be significant and should be distinguished from others. It is important to include estimates of supply costs even where the supply budget is not under the immediate jurisdiction of the media specialist. This is frequently a significant cost item, and is becoming even more so, and possibly a budget category should be made here (where it does not now exist) to facilitate more orderly and efficient planning.

Service outputs and unfilled request data. Service outputs and unfilled request data, which also are requested on this part of the "School Library/Media Program Data Collection Guide," are discussed separately later.

STAFF TIME DATA

A record for a sample of days of staff time spent on the various operations related to each service category should be maintained. Part II of the "School Library/Media Program Data Collection Guide" identifies the data to collect on the use of staff time in relation to each service subcategory. Key or illustrative operational tasks that are relevant to a specific service output category are listed. An operational task is defined as an intermediary task or job performed by the staff so that a service can ultimately be delivered—for example, materials processing, for which the ultimate service output would be circulation or in-the-center use. Use of time by the various individual staff members will have to be sampled where the percent of the staff member's time in relation to each service category is not readily apparent. In most cases some sampling of time will be necessary except where a staff member's total time or a clear percentage, such as 25 percent, is spent on one activity, such as processing. Record each staff member's time separately in each appropriate category with an identifying symbol, for example, "P2" for professional number two and "A" for the aide. The objective, however accomplished, is to establish reasonably accurate estimates of the percent of time spent annually by each staff member on each appropriate service subcategory.

Sampling. Where sampling is necessary, the sampling period is the number of days the staff will record how its time is spent. In general, the size of the sample is a function of the reliability desired, number of working days in a year, homogeneity of the various days in terms of seasonal or cyclic activities, the manner in which activities and operations are organized and records already maintained, and time available. As a rule-of-thumb, a twenty-day sample should suffice if it is spread over a sufficient period to capture most of the variations. Sampling can be discontinued when figures display a consistent pattern and/or confidence of accuracy is achieved. Since the media staff is intimately involved and familiar with the operations and activities, as well as time patterns, the more extensive sampling should be restricted to activities or service subcategories which occur irregularly or intermittently, making it difficult to estimate time spent on the activity. An example is the provision of identification and location assistance, which probably occurs frequently but takes only a small amount of time and is interspersed among a variety of other activities. Keeping track of time spent on various activities is difficult for some and easy for others, but it does take time. As a result, sampling should continue only as long as is necessary, and estimates which initially appear inaccurate or strange may be rechecked later.[4]

Selection of sample days. The days that are picked in the sample should be representative of the whole year. The sample should include days at the beginning, middle, and end of each semester, plus summers (where applicable), plus some representative days of the work week. Moreover, special days when unusual activities, such as the writing of annual reports or the taking of inventory, should be included if possible, although not so many as to bias the sample. However, if the specific amount of time for a special activity (such as taking inventory) is known, a sampling is not necessary since the percent of the total time devoted to this activity can be easily calculated for each staff member involved.

One could construct a list or calendar of all working days in the year and arbitrarily pick twenty days from that list. For example, one could pick every ninth day and go down the list until the twenty days are picked. Then the sample should be checked to be sure that some special activity days have been included, as well as days throughout the work week and throughout the work year.

Data collection. Each staff member can be asked to keep a diary or log and individually record the amount of time he or she spent in each sample day on each operational task. A simple but rather detailed record could be kept of what is actually done in terms of activities, or, if the individual is familiar with the service subcategories, the time spent could be recorded by these categories. The latter approach saves time because the data do not have to be translated into the service subcategories as a second step, since that is already accomplished. If it is too difficult to keep track of all the service subcategories at one time while one is collecting time data, another approach is to divide the services into reasonable clusters and record only the time spent on one group or cluster of services at one time and sample the other groups of services on different days. This would involve sampling on more days, but at least initially, and until one becomes thoroughly familiar with the service and operational categories, it may be easier to handle.

In numerous cases it is possible simply to stop every hour or half hour on the sample day and estimate the time spent on various activities and the number of times a specific service or operational activity occurred. However, on the other extreme, it may be necessary to have someone else (a volunteer, aide, or student) observe the media specialist performing certain activities because they may be difficult to capture through self-observation. Probably the most difficult example is that of providing identification and location assistance, because of the problems mentioned previously. A count must be kept of how frequently this occurs in the given time period, which is recorded as a service output figure, and the proportion of time expended during the period of this activity must be recorded. The observer can do this if the media specialist cannot, because of the intermittent and frequent nature as well as short duration of this service activity.

A similar problematic example is general supervision of the use of the center ("I. Access to Materials, Equipment, and Space; C. Provision of Space"), which refers to the activities necessary to keep things under reasonable control. Here only the time spent speaking to individuals or the whole group (whatever the case may be) is recorded as time spent on supervision. Simple "presence," when one is simultaneously doing something else (for example, reviewing potential materials selections), would not be recorded under supervision but under the operational task of selection ("I. Access to Materials, Equipment, and Space; A. Provision of Material"). However, time spent on supervising other media staff (for example, training, troubleshooting, and reviewing performance) is credited under the service subcategory of the work being supervised (supervising circulation procedures, for example, "I. Access to Materials, Equipment, and Space; D. Use of Materials, Equipment, and Space") and should not be confused with general supervision.

Activities which do not specifically or reasonably relate to any one service subcategory (for example, some management functions, such as overall planning or the act of collecting this time and other data) can be handled in a number of ways. The simplest method is to establish a miscellaneous category for management and to record the time in this category. This approach would in effect establish an overhead category and is not recommended, because the effort is to relate as many costs as possible to service outputs. Since these kinds of activities are necessary for implementation of all the services, the suggested method is to keep track of this time separately so that one has a good picture of the proportion of time that is spent on these activities. This is recorded in a miscellaneous management category which is carefully defined, but this time should also be divided proportionately over all the service subcategories where time is spent. This can most easily be accomplished by excluding this time when calculating the daily average of time spent on the various service categories. Then, by subtracting this amount of time from the total time sampled in that day or days, one has in effect distributed this time as desired. This relates as many of the costs as possible to the relevant service output categories.

It is recommended that the time be recorded in minutes. Division of the number of minutes spent on each activity or service subcategory by the number of minutes in an average working day (not including breaks) will yield the percentage of time spent on each activity. The work day should be interpreted as the number of paid hours, such as seven or eight hours in the normal working day—whatever is the case. Time spent over and above this amount is recorded in hours, as explained later in this discussion. It should be stressed that reasonable approximations rather than split-second accuracy are suitable.

After completing the time sampling for the number of days desired, each member of the media program staff can calculate a daily average for each appropriate service subcategory, based on averaging the time from all of the days sampled. If the averages are expressed in minutes, division by the total average minutes in a day or total minutes sampled should be carried out to express them as percentages for recording on the "School Library/ Media Program Costing Matrix."

Yearly average. The daily average must be converted into a yearly average. Any daily average that seems, in the best professional judgment of a media staff member, to be a reasonable estimate of the yearly percentage of time spent in the processing task in question should be considered as the yearly average. If the daily average seems biased, a subjective correction can be used in stating the yearly average *if* it can be justified. The major justification would be that the sample did not adequately reflect the situation, especially for special days when unusual or seasonal activities took place. If adjustments are made, the other time percentages in other categories will have to be adjusted so that the total time does not exceed 100 percent.

Contributed labor. Time spent by media staff on non-media program activities should be kept track of separately, and a record of time spent beyond normal working hours should also be documented. Time spent on non-media program activities (playground supervision, for example) will be recorded as a percentage of the total annual staff time available that must be devoted to such activities and, therefore, not to the media program. This is very common, and possibly a reasonable expectation of any school staff member if the amount of time *is* reasonable. This time should not be charged to the media program, however, since this would distort the amount and cost of labor expended to accomplish the media services.

It is also useful to document this time, if the amount is becoming unreasonable, in order to help make the case for restoring this lost labor to the media program. This should be recorded as a percent of total staff time at the end of the "School Library/Media Program Data Collection Guide" and "School Library/Media Program Costing Matrix" in a note. The total percent should always total 100—no more and no less—with the possibility that part of this total percentage is not devoted to media activities.

Time spent beyond normal working hours should be recorded in terms of average number of such hours required per year, but no cost is calculated for such time. These hours should be recorded as a separate item with the percent of paid time in the appropriate service subcategories, for example, with time spent on selection ("I. Access to Materials, Equipment, and Space; A. Provision of Materials") if this was how the time was spent.

Unpaid student and volunteer time should also be recorded with the appropriate symbol (S–500 hours) in terms of the average number of hours per year by the service subcategories where the time was spent. This is also contributed labor, used to accomplish the program of services, and should be recorded and communicated as such.

Salaries. The salaries of all media program personnel should be obtained so that they can be recorded on the "School Library/Media Program Costing Matrix" for calculating labor costs.

SERVICE OUTPUT DATA

The service output data that are of interest are the number of times per day, on the average, a specific media program service is given to users. One should collect in-center usage separately from out-of-center usage of services, where this distinction applies, and record these as two separate, appropriately identified numbers. One can also specify for each user group (for example, students by grade level or teachers by department) how often a given service output was used if those data are available and/or desired. If output data have been recorded for a specific service in "Part I: Physical Resources and Services Data" of the "School Library/Media Program Data Collection Guide" (for example, "I. Access to Materials, Equipment, and Space; A. Provision of Materials"), do not duplicate those output data in "Part II: Staff Time and Services Data" of the "School Library/Media Program Data Collection Guide" since this would be needless duplication. Service output data are the record of the frequency of use of each of the services and thus could be described as a record of the achievements or accomplishments of the media program for a given year. As a result, these are possibly the most important data to collect and report. Since these data reflect the performance of the media program, it is important that all service use be reported and not simply that service use which is traditionally or easily recorded, for example, circulation statistics. Part of clients' common unawareness of the variety of services offered is undoubtedly due to lack of recording and reporting the total range of services performed.

Sampling. A sample of days in the year, which could overlap with the time study sample discussed previously, should be selected in the same manner as explained under time sampling. However, a sample of thirty days is recommended here so that every sixth day is selected—going down the list of working days in the year. The larger sample is suggested in order to achieve greater reliability for this very important category of data. Judgment should be used to determine the desirability and feasibility of the number of days sampled to achieve the level of accuracy warranted, but a sample should be used, rather than spending exorbitant amounts of time on exhaustive data collection.

Data collection. A log of service outputs is recorded for each specific service for each day in the sample. It is very important to describe, through notes on the form, exactly what is meant by the output figures. Some service categories are very explicit (for example, provision of a specific kind of material) whereas others need amplification (for example, "II. Reference Services; D. Alerting the User and Current Awareness Services") in terms of just what is done in terms of the local media program. The elaborations or brief descriptors can frequently be listed in the appropriate box in the operational task column and the output figure recorded in the service output column. All notes should also be duplicated on the "School Library/Media Program Costing Matrix" so that misinterpretations do not occur.

In-center use figures are collected separately from out-of-center use figures for each service output. "In-center use" refers to the number of times a service output, such as a reference question responded to or a book or piece of equipment used, is delivered or transpired in the center itself. "Out-of-center use" refers to the number of times a service output, such as a book or piece of circulated equipment, is provided for use outside the center. For example, circulation records (which are also collected on a sample basis) can be used to obtain out-of-center service output data for materials and equipment. Special counts will likely have to be carried out for the "II. Reference Services," "III. Production Services," "IV. Instruction," and "V. Consulting Service" categories, as well as for some of the subcategories under "I. Access to Materials, Equipment, and Space." Thus a media staff member, in providing in-service training for teachers, must keep track of how often this was done during the days of the sample. Note that in-center use, traditionally a problem to measure, can be obtained by direct observation by using a no-shelving policy for the sample period and then counting the items to be reshelved (for example, material left on tables) or questioning clients on what they used by developing a simple form to be used for this purpose as they leave the center during the sample days. Simple forms, asking clients to record use with simple check marks, can also be placed with equipment or resources or facilities, as in viewing or listening rooms or carrels.

Some kinds of in-center use data can be easily collected by the person who performs the service when the time data are collected. For example, the occurrence of many reference, production, instruction, and consulting services could just as easily be recorded at the same time the time estimates are collected and recorded.

The arrangement of the media center will greatly influence how in-center use occurs and, as a result, how data will have to be collected. In fact, it is impossible to prescribe general data collection strategies that will apply in every situation. Local strategies will have to be generated to develop estimates of in-center use of a center's resources in many cases, but various adaptations of the techniques (only suggested here) should make it possible to calculate reasonable estimates of this important category of services. The most traditional measure of in-center use has been a simple head count of the people who use the center in a given period (this would be recorded as an output figure under "I. Access to Materials, Equipment, and Space; C. Provision of Space") However, this is a weak and ineffective means of representing in-center use and should be used only in addition to the previously mentioned use data, if at all possible, and only to indicate the amount of "traffic flow" the center is accommodating.[5]

Note also that one counts number of service outputs, as opposed to number of people exposed to a media service. For example, an overhead projector that is lent to a teacher is *one* usage of that piece of equipment, although perhaps thirty people were exposed to its use or the teacher may have used it with five classes. If one wants to keep exposure counts, that is fine if it is done separately and in addition to the basic output data. In fact, in the example used, keeping track of the number of classes with which the projector was used may provide a more expressive use figure. This kind of data is usually collected by having a teacher indicate the number of times used (specifically defined) on a simple form that is supplied with the equipment. This may not be the most accurate way of collecting use data, but it provides a reasonable basis for better estimates of use in a relatively cheap manner.

Yearly average. The number of service outputs is averaged for the sample to yield an average daily figure for each specific service, which is then used to generate the yearly average output by multiplying the daily average output figure by the number of days in a year that the service is given.

Adjustments can also be made in the yearly average output data, as was done with the yearly average time data (discussed earlier), but one should be very careful that artificially inflated figures do not result which provide a distorted and dishonest profile of media program accomplishments.

OPERATIONAL OUTPUT DATA

An operational output is an intermediate product that is generated as part of some processing activity (for example, reports written or items selected or processed). Data of special interest are the number of times per day that an operational output is generated. The data are gathered and averaged in exactly the same manner as for service outputs but are recorded in the operational output column of "Part II: Staff Time and Services Data" of the "School Library/Media Program Data Collection Guide."

Data should be gathered only for those operational outputs listed in the "School Library/Media Program Data Collection Guide" or those added outputs that may be useful in further analysis of the program in terms of the relative cost or efficiency of these operational tasks relative to services delivered or to other operational alternatives. Thus operational output data should be gathered only for operational tasks where one wants to test the efficiency of current methods and consider alternative methods, as discussed in chapter 6.

UNFILLED REQUEST DATA

An unfilled request is a demand for a specific service output that the media staff could not provide. These data are used to assess—with other data—the degree to which demands for service are satisfied. The data are collected in exactly the same manner as for service outputs. Only specific, expressed demands that remained unfilled are recorded. Again, the "School Library/Media Program Data Collection Guide" can be used to record the unfilled request data. These data will be analyzed and will provide additional documentation for the need for increased service capability by showing the potential demand from users for such new or increased services.

It is also possible, and useful, to record the expressed reasons for unfilled requests with symbols, such as "Lack of staff," "Lack of materials or equipment," "Lack of space," or, instead, to cite a school function or miscellaneous event that disturbed the flow of routine work. These data are obviously incomplete in that they inevitably reflect only a portion of unfilled needs. However, unfilled but expressed demands are useful indicators and documentation that demands exceed capabilities, or they may also indicate an area of inefficiency where operational procedures need review and revision. It is possible to assess unfilled demands or needs more com-

PHYSICAL RESOURCE ELEMENTS BY SERVICE SUBDIVISIONS	RESOURCE QUANTITIES				COSTS		SERVICE OUTPUTS		NUMBER OF UNFILLED REQUESTS*
	CURRENT HOLDINGS	NUMBER ITEMS REPLACED	NUMBER ITEMS ADDED	TOTAL NO. ITEMS PURCHASED	COST RANGE	AVERAGE UNIT COST	In Center	Out of Center	
A. PROVISION OF MATERIALS									
Materials									
(Books)									
Hardback	7,500	25	375	400	.60–45.00	6.06	9,875	6,122	495
Paperback	500	—	100	100	1.25–4.75	2.75	1,226	985	100
Large print, etc.									

* Number of unfilled requests: 495 = 125 titles and 370 items in circulation unavailable. 100 = 25 titles and 75 items in circulation unavailable.

Fig. 8. "Part I: Physical resources and services data (example) Service I: Access to materials, equipment, space"

SERVICE SUBDIVISIONS	OPERATIONAL TASKS	TIME	SAMPLE 1			SAMPLE 2, ETC.	DAILY AVERAGE* (IN %)	YEARLY AVERAGE* (IN %)
			SERVICE OUTPUTS	OPER-ATIONAL OUTPUTS	UNFILLED REQUESTS			
A. PROVISION OF MATERIALS	Processing materials	P1 20 min. P2 18 min. A 4 hrs. 38 min.		3 5 42		18 min. 20 min. 5 hrs.	4% 4 58	4% 4 58
	Selection and evaluation (new and replacement items)	P1 1 hr. 24 min P2 1 hr.		10 5		1 hr. 45 min.	15 15	15 15
	Maintenance of collection (inventory, reports, etc.)	reports P1 10min. P2 10min. inventory S-2 hrs. A-0				15 min. 10 min.	2 2	2 2 A-2

* The daily average is computed first by averaging the minutes spent on each operational task by each individual for all the days sampled. This average number of minutes is then divided by the total number of minutes in a day in order to compute the percent of time. Unpaid labor, for example students and adult volunteers, is represented in average number of hours rather than percent of time since costs are not calculated.
Hours available: Professional = 480 min./day   Aide = 420 min./day

Fig. 9. "Part II: Staff time and services data (example) Service I: Access to materials, equipment, space"

prehensively with user surveys specifically designed for this purpose. A common approach is to include a few additional questions regarding unfilled needs on the form used to collect in-center use data (suggested earlier). With this approach on these sample days, users are given the opportunity to express unfilled needs as well as indicate resources and services that actually are used.

Completed samples of "Part I: Physical Resources and Services Data" (see figure 8) and "Part II: Staff Time and Services Data" (see figure 9) of the "School Library/Media Program Data Collection Guide" are included to illustrate how the various kinds of data discussed in this chapter are represented and recorded.

Obviously, the collection of reliable and comprehensive data for systematic program planning is of critical importance, but it is also time consuming and probably less precise than one might wish. There is, however, no alternative, and the size of the task can be reduced considerably if the techniques for sampling and estimating are heeded. The most important principle is to relate as many of the cost factors as possible to the appropriate service subcategory and to be as consistent as possible in defining and categorizing things. The "School Library/Media Program Data Collection Guide" and the "School Library/Media Program Costing Matrix" are working tools or documents for the media staff and are typically filled with notations which describe or explain the local interpretation or use of terms and categories or operational tasks. This is to be encouraged to facilitate consistent interpretations and use of the data when they are recorded on the "School Library/Media Program Costing Matrix" and ultimately are used to accomplish the various program analysis and reporting functions described in the next chapter.

NOTES

1. Mary E. Crookston, *Unit Costs in a Selected Group of High School Libraries* (U.S. Office of Education, Bulletin no. 11, 1941), p. 5.

2. Constance Brutcher, Glen Gessford, and Emmet Rixford, "Cost Accounting for the Library," *Library Resources and Technical Services* 8:413–31 (Fall 1964).

3. Fred J. Heinritz, "Quantitative Management in Libraries," *College and Research Libraries* 31:234 (July 1970).

4. Some further suggestions for improved collection of time data and the determination of labor costs are included in Carol C. Spencer, "Random Time Sampling with Self-Observation for Li-

brary Cost Studies: Unit Costs of Interlibrary Loans and Photocopies at a Regional Medical Library," *Journal of the American Society for Information Science* 22:153–60 (May–June 1971).

5. Some further suggestions in this difficult area of measuring in-center use (as well as general use) can be found in William G. Jones, "A Time-Series Sample Approach for Measuring Use in a Small Library," *Special Libraries* 64:280–84 (July 1973), and A. K. Jain, "Sampling In-Library Book Use," *Journal of the American Society for Information Science* 2:150–55 (May–June 1972).

CHAPTER 6

Program Analysis

The variety of program data which have been collected (as described in previous chapters) is finally amalgamated in one convenient place, the "School Library/Media Program Costing Matrix," and is arranged in such a manner so as to reflect relationships and to expedite and encourage various kinds of systematic and analytical examinations of the program. The data previously collected must be recorded on the "School/Media Program Costing Matrix," if this has not been done directly (and where other data collection forms or records have been used).

The transfer of the data onto the "School Library/Media Program Costing Matrix" is very straightforward since the columns are the same, except that the data from both parts of the "School Library/Media Program Data Collection Guide" (see figure 8 and figure 9) are now merged under the service output subcategories. Each service subcategory, where appropriate, includes columns in two basic formats. The first format (see figure 10) is provided to accommodate all the material, equipment, and supply data for that service subcategory. The second format (see figure 11), immediately following the first and preceding the listing of the next service subcategory, is provided to accommodate staff time and service data. Where both formats are included, the service output data are normally recorded in the column labeled "Service and Operational Outputs," in the materials and so forth section of the form for that service subcategory, and the operational outputs are included in the staff time section. The only new data required are salary data, to make it possible to calculate time costs and, ultimately, total service and program costs, including all direct labor, materials, equipment, and supply costs.

After all the data, including the value or priority consensus data, derived in the group priority determination sessions, have been recorded on the "School Library/Media Program Costing Matrix" with the relevant notations and explanations, only a few rather simple computations are required to complete the form.

RESOURCE ELEMENTS BY SERVICE SUBDIVISIONS	RESOURCE QUANTITIES				COSTS			SERVICE AND OPERATIONAL OUTPUTS		UNFILLED REQUESTS*
	CURRENT HOLDINGS	ITEMS REPLACED	ITEMS ADDED	TOTAL ITEMS PURCHASED	COST RANGE	AVERAGE UNIT COST	PROGRAM (SERVICE) COST	In Center	Out of Center	
A. PROVISION OF MATERIALS										
Materials										
(Books)										
Hardback	7,500	25	375	400	.60 – 45.00	6.06	2,424.	9,875	6,122	495
Paperback	500	–	100	100	1.25 – 4.75	2.75	275.	1,226	985	100
Large print, etc.										

* Number of unfilled requests: 495 = 125 titles and 370 items in circulation unavailable. 100 = 25 titles and 75 items in circulation unavailable.

Fig. 10. Program costing matrix (example 1) "Service I: Access to materials, equipment, space"

RESOURCE ELEMENTS BY SERVICE SUBDIVISIONS	RESOURCE QUANTITIES		COSTS		SERVICE AND OPERATIONAL OUTPUTS
	STAFF TIME		SALARY	PROGRAM (SERVICE) COSTS	
	OPERATIONAL TASKS	AMOUNT OF TIME			
A. PROVISION OF MATERIALS (cont.) *Staff*		p1 4% p2 4%	13,000 11,000	$ 520 440	[operational outputs]
	Processing materials	A 58%	5,000	2,900	950
	Selection and evaluation (new and replacement items)	p1 15% p2 15%	13,000 11,000	1,950 1,650	1,200
	Maintenance of collection (inventory, reports, etc.)	p1 2% p2 2% S 100 hrs. A 2%	13,000 11,000 5,000	260 220 100	reports to admin 1 annual 4 interim annual 1--inventory

* Salaries are on a ten-month basis: Aide—$5,000; Professional 1—$13,000; Professional 2—$11,000; Students—$0.00. Hours available are: Aide—(200 days/yr. x 7 hrs./day) = 1400 hrs.; Professional—(200 days/yr. x 8 hrs./day) = 1600 hrs.; Students (200 days/yr. x 10 hrs./day) = 2000 hrs.

Fig. 11. Program costing matrix (example 2) "Service I: Access to materials, equipment, space"

1. The costs to be recorded in each appropriate box in the "Program (Service) Cost" column of materials, equipment, or supplies are computed by multiplying the total number of items purchased that year by the average unit cost of the item, or by simply recording the amount expended for the year for that item, if that information is readily available.[1]

2. The costs of staff time for every staff member for each operational task in each service subcategory are computed by multiplying the salary by the percent of average yearly time spent on that item.

3. The subtotals for which summary tables are provided at the end of each service subcategory (see figure 12) are simply computed by adding

Materials Costs	$ 3,757
Supply Costs	450
Staff Costs	8,040
A. PROVISION OF MATERIALS COSTS	$12,247

Fig. 12. Service subcategory summary table (example)

all materials, equipment, supplies, and staff costs separately, recording these totals, and then adding them all together to provide the total cost of all direct cost factors for each service subcategory.

4. The subtotals for each major service category (see figure 13) are then computed by simply adding together the total cost figures for each service subcategory. The same technique is then applied to compute the total program cost (see figure 14). These figures are recorded, in these two cases, in the column labeled "Total." The column labeled "Value in Percent" at this point would contain the values derived in step 3 of the planning process, translated into percentages to facilitate comparisons with costs, and the other two columns would be blank.

5. The staff costs for each subcategory and then each major category are also added together and recorded in the summary tables for each major service category and the total summary table for the five major categories at the end of the "School Library/Media Program Costing Matrix." This is done to facilitate the computation of percent of staff costs expended on each service category and subcategory distinctly and separately from the total cost, where time costs are combined with physical resource costs.

	STAFF ONLY	TOTAL	PERCENT OF TOTAL COST STAFF	PERCENT OF TOTAL COST TOTAL	VALUE (IN PERCENT)
A. Provision of Materials Costs	$ 8,040	$12,247	28%	36%	12%
B. Provision of Audiovisual Equipment Costs	220	1,021	1	3	8
C. Provision of Space Costs	1,060	1,060	4	3	4
D. Use of Materials, etc. Costs	2,440*	2,440	9	7	6
E. Provision of Materials Not in Collection Costs					1
F. Provision of Special Collections Costs	1,200	1,200	4	4	3
G. Copying Costs					1
I. ACCESS TO MATERIALS, EQUIPMENT, SPACE COSTS	$12,960	$17,968	46	53	35

* Some of this cost applies to subdivisions E, F, and G as well.

Fig. 13. Major service category summary table (example)

	STAFF ONLY	TOTAL	PERCENT OF TOTAL COST STAFF	PERCENT OF TOTAL COST TOTAL	VALUE (IN PERCENT)
I. ACCESS TO MATERIALS, EQUIPMENT, AND SPACE	$12,960	$17,968	46%	53%	35%
II. REFERENCE SERVICES	7,130	7,730	25	23	15
III. PRODUCTION SERVICES	990	1,104	3.5	3	15
IV. INSTRUCTION	5,520	5,520	19.5	16	25
V. CONSULTING SERVICES	1,680	1,680	6	5	10
Total	$28,280	$34,002			

Fig. 14. Total program (service) costs summary table (example)

6. The dollar costs in the final and service subcategory summary tables are then translated into percent of total cost figures to provide the basis for beginning to apply the comparison and analysis strategies (discussed later). It is recommended that *both* the percent of total program cost and the percent of total staff cost be computed for the major service categories and the subcategories. Both of these percentages would be recorded in separate columns within the "Percent of Total Cost" column. The percent of total program cost figures are computed by dividing the total program cost figure, indicated on the bottom line of the "Total Program (Service) Costs" summary table, into—first—each subtotal cost figure for each major service category (see figure 14) and then into each subtotal cost figure for the service subcategories (see figure 13). The same approach is used to compute the percent of total staff costs, except that the "staff only" total (see figure 14) is divided into the "staff only" subtotals, first for each major category and then for each subcategory, as before. When these percentages are computed, the instrument is complete and the analysis may begin.

Program Analysis Strategies

Once the program data have been collected and recorded in the format suggested, almost innumerable kinds of analyses and uses of the data are possible. The following strategies are intended only to serve as a very basic guide to the most fundamental kinds of analyses and are suggestive of other kinds of analyses and uses which can be applied and elaborated on in each local situation. The kinds of analyses suggested can be performed at different times, and frequently, if not inevitably, lead to the collection of additional data in areas identified as problem areas and to the continuing collection of some kinds of data for evaluation, needs assessment, accountability, and annual or more frequent reporting purposes. Further sampling, scheduled over time, can always be done to improve the reliability of data where they initially appear shaky upon analysis and to provide a constantly current picture of service accomplishments, stewardship of resources, and so forth.

REALLOCATIONS

The objective of this analysis strategy is to investigate the current use of resources (time and physical resources) to determine whether a more effective match between preferred services and the services currently delivered can be achieved with current resources. The service value percentages are compared against the percent of total program cost for particular services and the percent of total staff time for particular services. The additional comparison with percent of staff time is made because the allocation of staff time is the factor most capable of being manipulated and controlled by the media staff in planning and implementing media services. The costs of materials, equipment, and supplies are fixed, in that these items generally cannot be reallocated or converted into other service categories, whereas staff time can be reallocated to almost any service category. By reallocating staff time, therefore, one can make significant changes in the configuration of services offered, and thus comparing service values with staff time allocations, in addition to total resource allocations, is a particularly useful technique in calculating potential program changes. This, therefore, is one means of analyzing the *effectiveness* of the program.

A word of caution should be expressed at this point about the use of "judgment" in comparing and equating cost and value considerations. The precise relationship that should exist between cost and value in any given instance is not known and a perfect match may be impossible. The purpose of making the comparisons is simply to assist the staff in carefully analyzing the program in terms of effectiveness (satisfactorily serving client needs) and efficiency (achieving the most output with a given amount of input or resources). Therefore a discrepancy between value and cost forces the professional to review this situation to determine if the discrepancy can be adequately explained or—hopefully—to consider alternative arrangements which would reduce the discrepancy. The point is that these numbers or quantities are representational only, and frequently not very precise, and therefore should not be substituted for professional judgment. The simple manipulation of numbers without careful and serious regard for the substantive and frequently complex phenomena they represent, as well as the implications of the decisions made on this basis, would be foolhardy and a serious misuse of these techniques. The basic steps and sequence to follow in performing this kind of analysis are as follows.

Compare values and use of resources. Review, on the last page of the "School Library/Media Program Costing Matrix," the values for each of the five major service categories as compared to the percent of resources currently allocated to each category. Look for major discrepancies between total program cost percentages and total staff cost percentages compared to service value percentages. For example, "I. Access to Materials, Equipment, and Space" may have a value of 35 percent but a total cost of 65 percent and a total staff cost of 53 percent. For another example, "II. Reference Services" might have a total value of 20 percent but a total cost of 8 percent and a total staff cost of 5 percent. Make a note of all major discrepancies.

Review subcategories. Perform the same kind of review of each service subcategory in each summary table at the end of each major service category, and also make a note of major discrepancies.

Consider possible and alternative reallocations. Consider possible and alternative reallocations of resources (materials and equipment where possible but most frequently staff time) from those major categories and subcategories with much higher cost than value, which should lose resources ("I. Access to Materials, Equipment and Space" in the example), to those categories with much lower cost than value, which should gain resources ("II. Reference Services" in the example). Determination of which categories are to gain and which are to lose is not difficult. The problems come in determining how much of a gain or loss for each category should be considered and in determining how to effect such a shift in resources. Moreover, a change in resources for a major service category does not always mean proportional changes in the subcategories of service under that category. For example, a decrease in resources for a major category, "I. Access to Materials, Equipment, and Space," may be considered with a corresponding decrease in resources in a subcategory, "A. Provision of Materials." However, resources in the subcategory "C. Provision of Space" might remain constant, and resources for "B. Provision of Audiovisual Equipment" might even be increased.

Consider incremental changes. Large shifts in resources, when broken down into a series of smaller reallocation changes spread over time, allow one to test if the direction and amount of change is possible and desirable in terms of improved program effectiveness. This approach may also help to minimize the shock to clients and staff of a sudden change and to test the accuracy of client values by getting feedback regarding those services where service outputs are actually reduced by the reallocations. Moreover, this allows time to search for the best balance between value and cost and to provide the documentation to substantiate this relationship.

For categories to be increased, users must be informed of the new services to ensure that demand for them will be realized. In such cases, increases may be implemented incrementally, so that service capability does not grossly exceed actual demands or use of the service. Very frequently, users require a "taste" of the new service before they can place a value on it or make adequate use of it. This also may be partial justification for offering a service for which no demand has been expressed—at least on a pilot basis and in conjunction with some in-service or orientation activities.

Estimate reallocation performance targets. Estimate reallocation performance targets or specific amounts of increases in resources for each service subcategory that deserves an increase. Details on the current use of resources in each subcategory should be examined in the "School Library/Media Program Costing Matrix" (see figures 10 and 11). Consider how much staff time, materials, equipment, and supplies are required to produce the current output. Generate estimates of desired output levels (program performance targets), based on the percent of increase indicated by the values and unfilled request data. Generate estimates of how many more resources are needed to achieve those desired service output levels (program performance targets), based on proportionate increases over what amounts of resources are required to support current output levels.[2]

Determine whether increases in efficiency, or eliminating or refining operations and procedures and thereby reducing the resources required to produce current output, can produce extra resources to help provide the desired output levels (program performance targets). The instructions for analyzing efficiency are discussed below. Also determine if some aspects of a service or conditions under which a service is offered may be eliminated or reduced in order to produce extra resources. The values assigned to the arabic number and small-letter services on the "Form for Determining Preferences for School Library/Media Center Services" should be of help in evaluating these kinds of alternatives.

Output is really a response to a demand from clients for service. A cutback in some service categories may require turning down expressed demands. Caution and judgment must be exercised in such service categories. A low value and high cost may justify a cutback; however, in a subcategory such as "I. Access to Materials, Equipment, and Space; A. Provision of Materials," demand may increase even though it was given a low value. This demand may be a more accurate expression of value than the client preferences and, therefore, possibly should not be reduced; and the value should be reassessed. In categories such as "II. Reference Services" or "III. Production Services," an increase in resources allows for a capability to deliver more service outputs, but this capability may not be used initially if the demand is not there. Gradual increases in such categories, particularly in terms of the allocation of time, should definitely be considered. Demands for some services may also indicate a need for other services; for example, increased demands for identification and location assistance may indicate a need for increased instructional services. In such a case, a specifically planned instructional program may be considered as a means of reducing the demands for assistance services, and the resulting effects on the demand for assistance may be used to measure the effectiveness of the instruction. This kind of approach may also be considered as a means of reducing demands in high-cost but lower-priority service areas.

Estimate decreases. Estimate the decreases in resources for each service subcategory that deserves a decrease. Using a parallel approach to the one outlined above in estimating reallocation targets for increases, examine the details regarding the current use of resources in each subcategory in the "School Library/Media Program Costing Matrix." Consider how much of each resource is required to produce the current service outputs.[3] Generate estimates of possible output level reductions (which then become program performance targets), based on values and current demand. Estimate amounts of resources that can be saved by cutting back on service outputs.

Consider whether increases in efficiency can produce extra savings in low value–high cost subcategories. Output may not have to be reduced as much if the operational tasks can be made more efficient or low-value aspects of a service are eliminated or reduced.

Consider the net effect. Consider the net effect on each major service category of resource allocations in the subcategories. Reexamine the reallocations to ensure that the effect on the program and on each major category is desirable in terms of the initial reallocation considerations discussed previously. Determine the operational and procedural changes that are necessary to accomplish the program performance targets with appropriate staff members and the plans for implementing them.

If the reallocations are planned for a one-year trial period (which is very common practice), establish interim check points when operational progress and client use and responses are assessed and appropriate modifications are made. Also, where operational changes have been made, these changes should be carefully monitored to assess whether increased efficiency has been achieved or the quality of service has diminished to an undesirable degree.

ANALYZING EFFICIENCY

The process of analyzing reallocation possibilities was intentionally designed to increase interest and motivation in assessing the efficiency of media program operational tasks and routines. One means of finding additional resources is to find better methods of producing current service outputs which require less time or cost. This means increasing efficiency. For example, could certain processing routines be refined, replaced, or eliminated in order to reduce the time and therefore cost per item? If one has collected data on operational outputs—in this case the number of items processed per year—one can calculate, by dividing the number of items processed into the total annual cost of this operational task (percent of time spent times salaries), a unit cost for processing one item.[4] By comparing this figure with similar figures in other programs, or by making a judgment regarding the reasonableness of this figure, one can begin to identify areas where efficiency may be increased; and by repeating this process periodically, one can measure rather precisely the progress being made toward improved efficiency. Resources that are saved on inefficient or less important operations can obviously be used elsewhere to improve program effectiveness. Some general suggestions to accomplish this are as follows.

Identify operations to be analyzed. Identify those operations or tasks performed by staff members that should be analyzed. Concentrate on high-cost or time-consuming operations—especially those related to services with low values and those where values are substantially lower than staff-time costs.

Examine the types of changes. Examine the types of changes that might make an operation more efficient.

Can an operation or routine be eliminated?

Can an operation or routine be cut back without lowering the quality or level of service output?

Can an operation be delegated to less expensive personnel, as from a professional staff member to a paraprofessional or clerical staff member or from a clerical staff member to a volunteer?

Can procedures be improved or replaced to reduce the time and/or cost of an operation?

Can an operation be centralized or sent out to be done by a commercial firm?

Some of these changes may require additional resources to be studied and/or implemented. Some may be best undertaken in phases over a period of time, or tried out for a test period, before a full commitment is made to changeover.

It is important to note that cutbacks and elimination of some operations may not be very desirable but may be better than not being able to increase high-value services. The tradeoffs should be carefully considered in these cost/benefit terms. Simply becoming more time conscious can result in increased efficiency and more explicitly considered performance. The development of operational and procedural manuals and performance standards or targets and guides can be a healthy outcome of this kind of analysis and result in not only more efficient but more consistent performance.

Specify the types and amounts of change. For each operation to be changed, specify the types and amounts of change. Generate estimates of the resources to be saved by each change. The total savings should also be calculated. Resource savings should be considered not only in terms of overall cost but also in terms of the amounts of materials, equipment, supplies, and staff time to be saved and reallocated.

JUSTIFICATION

The justification of resource requests is becoming increasingly more demanding and critical. The point cannot be overemphasized that even where annual reporting and/or submission of budget justification data is not formally required, it is strongly recommended that this be done in order to educate administrators and provide data they can use in preparing their budget justifications and requests. In this light, a small amount of data can go a long way toward making these representations more convincing. It is critical in making justification representations that a sound strategy be used in laying the groundwork for specific resource requests. The best groundwork is a solid and systematic evaluation of the media program, such as that suggested here. A few suggestions for constructing resource requests and justifications are as follows.

Present concrete documentation of accountability and stewardship. Express the rationale and background for a request with as much concrete documentation of accountability as possible. The predilections of individual administrators are important to consider and should influence the manner and detail of the representation.

First, the current achievements or performance of the media program should be clearly documented in terms of the variety and scale of service outputs being delivered. The output data in the "School Library/Media Program Costing Matrix" will be useful here.

Second, the current resources required to provide the service outputs of the program should be summarized—what it takes to maintain the current program. The data on materials, equipment, supplies, and staff-time costs, in the "School Library/Media Program Costing Matrix," will be useful here. The costs and operational requirements of media services, to say the very least, are very poorly understood by administrators (among others). Effective reporting of this information on at least an annual basis is therefore essential.

Third, program changes that are made by reallocation to increase program effectiveness should be documented. Also, program operational changes, made to increase efficiency, should be documented. One must be certain that no further resources can be generated by reallocation or increased efficiency. In effect, what one is doing here is documenting one's stewardship and effectiveness.

Provide for the justification of additional resources. One can now calculate needs beyond what are possible with current resources, and provide justification for the resources required to respond to those needs. Consider high priority service subcategories that require increased resources to improve program effectiveness. Identify service subcategories where additional resources are needed to increase the quality and level of service outputs to the level indicated by client preference and unfilled request data.

Determine the amounts of additional resources needed. For subcategories where increased resources are needed, determine the amount of additional resources required to generate the desired increase in service output levels. The desired output levels, based on values, current outputs, and unfilled request data, must be calculated first. Then, based on the proportionate increases over what amounts of resources are required to support current output levels, the additional resources needed to bring the output levels up to the desired levels must be calculated and represented as resource requests.

REDUCTIONS

Reductions in resources are, unfortunately, becoming more frequent. The process for planning a reduced program fairly and effectively is similar to the reallocation process, and the following procedures could be followed.

1. Identify the amount of reduction in each resource category.
2. Considering current output and value data, specify which service subcategories could be cut back and document the implications. Look first at the high cost–low value subcategories. Unfilled request data can also be helpful.
3. Determine the amount to be cut back in each subcategory, following the same procedures as in determining reallocations.
4. Determine the resource savings from the service cutbacks, in terms of specific resources and time and in terms of cost.
5. Compare the savings with the necessary reductions. If more reduction is needed, reconsider procedure 3 in this harsher light. If the savings exceed the required resource reductions, consider a reallocation of the excess.
6. Be sure that considerations of reallocation and efficiency are not left out when seeking ways to cut back service.
7. Document reduction results and implications by collecting unfilled request data, particularly in those areas, and any other expressions of unfilled needs that can be generated. Consider reassessing client values after reductions have been implemented for a period of time, since reduced services may influence different patterns of use, and carefully evaluate the efficiency of operations (as previously suggested).
8. Reporting the results and user implications of reductions is essential and should be presented to as many different school and parent groups as can be arranged.

The stress in the program analysis strategies suggested here is on systematic and continuous planning and both formative and summative program evaluation.[5] Regular collection of program data on a sampling basis and judicious preparation of effective reports, based on careful analysis and evaluation of these data, should provide a reasonably solid basis for development and communication of accountable and effective media programs.

A program adapted to local circumstances and effectively responsive to the needs of aware clients, however, is the ultimate "proof of the pudding."

NOTES

1. In the case of supply costs, an estimate of the costs can be calculated, even if they are not a part of the media center budget, by keeping records of kinds and quantities of supplies used for different service categories and obtaining cost figures from central-office catalogues or personnel. Usually, however, only a lump sum is recorded in the "Program (Service) Cost" column, with a footnote explaining what is included.

2. Another method of analyzing or estimating specific relationships between service outputs and the amounts of resources needed to provide them is the calculation of unit costs. The unit cost for a service subcategory is calculated by dividing the total cost for that subcategory by the number of service outputs in that subcategory. The total cost includes materials costs, equipment costs, supplies costs, and staff-time costs. If the total cost for "Answer Services" was $500 for fifty service outputs, the unit cost is $10. Of course, this is a rough estimate of unit cost and a more detailed analysis can be carried out as needed. The use of mate-

rials, supplies, equipment, and especially staff time should also be noted separately. Thus one has estimates of how much materials, equipment, supplies, and staff time are required to produce a unit of output for a specific service subcategory. Changes in allocation of staff time can, in some categories, accomplish a significant change and may not involve reallocating other resources. This method may be tried where a more detailed or specific understanding of the resource requirement of various service output levels is desired. This same procedure can be applied to the calculation of unit costs for operational outputs.

3. Ibid.

4. Ibid.

5. An elaboration of the close relationship between planning and evaluation, as well as various approaches to evaluation supportive of the techniques suggested here, is Ernest R. DeProspo and James W. Liesener, "Media Program Evaluation: A Working Framework," *School Media Quarterly* 3:289–301 (Summer 1975).

CHAPTER 7

Implementing the Planning Process

There are no absolutes, to the writer's knowledge, for the "right" or best ways to introduce systematic planning techniques that are compatible with all conceivable local circumstances. The intent in the development of this planning process was to provide techniques which could be implemented in different ways, at different times, and on different scales. A considered examination of the local situation in terms of potential receptivity, responsiveness, constraints, and problems should be an important part of the initial preparations, which might be referred to as the "planning-to-plan stage."

A number of factors should be considered when one is beginning the planning for the application of this process and these techniques. A definite and serious commitment is necessary if the process is to be fully completed and the results utilized. Certain aspects of planning, such as data collection, are rather tedious and intrusive into normal daily routines. Moreover, the payoff of seeing and using the results is delayed for quite a period of time. Some individual or collective reinforcement is useful periodically to sustain interest and momentum, such as monthly (or more frequent) reporting of progress and discussion of problems among staff, or, if at all possible, with media staff in other schools who are also introducing or implementing planning techniques. District-level media staff, where they exist, can also be very supportive. This helps to establish specific objectives and target dates for completion of tasks and provides interim satisfaction of accomplishment, as well as an orderly sequence of steps progressing toward a foreseeable end.

Probably the most common problem is the dedication of time to planning. Staff time, as well as some client time at certain points, is definitely required and should be calculated and firmly committed in advance. Obviously, such arrangements as released time and additional assistance would be extremely helpful and should be requested, but in most cases time will likely have to be taken from other activities. The strategy for finding this time can be much the same as that suggested in the previous chapter in considering strategies for reallocating resources and increasing efficiency. The decision, however, will ultimately involve considerations of the value or priority of program planning as opposed to the value of other uses of staff time.

The question could be asked: Can a professional, performing a service function such as that of a media specialist, afford not to spend at least some time on careful needs assessment, program planning, and evaluation? In the writer's view, the inherent operational complexity of media programs, the variety and extent of client needs, the range of alternative service responses, and the potential for discrimination and unfairness, as well as inefficient or ineffective use of resources, are factors which suggest, and possibly demand, that time be devoted to systematically planning and managing media programs.

Alternative Approaches

Several different basic approaches may be used to begin implementation. Part of the planning process (internal data collection, for example) involves only the media staff and could therefore be started on a rather small scale and extended over time without encountering the logistical and other problems involved with surveying users' awareness and service needs. This is a common approach, and it enables the media staff to develop a clear picture of the operation of the media program prior to collecting data on client perceptions and preferences.

The reverse approach is also possible and is frequently used. Here one begins by assessing user awareness and needs and follows up (at a later time) with the internal data collection. This strategy enables one to begin immediately to develop a clear picture of user needs and awareness. It also begins the planning process in a logical fashion by concentrating on increasing user awareness and actively involving users in determining the services they are to receive.

A third and more ambitious alternative would be to start simultaneously with both of these approaches—which is perfectly possible but may involve the commitment of more time in an intensive manner. It is possible, in the third approach, to sequence activities over a longer period, such as a year or two, so that unreasonable amounts of time are not required at any one time. This approach permits reporting back to clients the full analysis of the program without the long time interval between collecting the data and reporting back the full results and implications.

Any of these approaches may also be implemented in two phases, with the first phase run as a pilot experiment, using very small samples of clients in a survey and needs assessment and also small samples of each kind of data in the "School Library/Media Program Data Collection Guide." This enables one to work out problems and procedures on a small scale before moving into the second phase, where more individuals are involved and larger samples of data are collected. This also provides the opportunity to do at least some program analysis and to identify areas where further study might be particularly useful.

Implementation Sequence and Participation

The sequencing of planning activities (detailed in previous chapters), including the specification of who might be involved in different ways, is illustrated in figure 15. Some of these activities must be performed sequentially, for example, steps 2, 5, 6, and 10 in conducting the survey with the "Inventory of School Library/Media Center Services." However, data collection (step 3), using the "School Library/Media Program Data Collection Guide," could be done anytime, but must be completed in order to do the program analysis (step 11).

A preliminary activity—prior to meeting with the principal in step 1— would be consideration by the media staff of the planning process and preparation of an explanation of the process and the reasons for wanting to use it, as well as a tentative implementation plan. It is important to include in the explanation such things as expected involvement of clients, suggested scheduling and time estimates of projected group sessions, and requests for whatever assistance or approval is needed for such things as the use of in-service days for group priority-determination sessions. These suggestions are meant to give the administrator a clear picture of what is involved so that approval is not given without full realization of what is intended and required. At this point it would also be useful to obtain approval for, and suggestions regarding, the makeup of an advisory committee to assist in planning and implementing the various activities. An advisory committee can be extremely useful in obtaining client support and assistance, but more importantly in establishing this planning effort as a mutual and collective endeavor.

The implementation plan, developed by the media staff and reviewed by the principal and the advisory committee, should detail—in terms of a one- or two- year plan—when each activity or step in the planning process will occur, who will be involved and with what specific responsibilities, the scale of each activity (indicating such things as estimated sample size of the survey and the number of days various kinds of data will be collected,

	MEDIA STAFF	PRINCIPAL	ADVISORY COM-MITTEE	STUDENT COUNCIL	TEACHERS	STUDENTS	TEACHER SAMPLE	STUDENT SAMPLE
1. Explanation and Decision	C	P						
2. Orientation, *Inventory, Preference*	C	P	P					
3. Begin Data Collection	C							
4. General Orientation	C	A	A	P	P			
5. Select *Inventory* and *Preference* Samples	C	A	A	A				
6. *Inventory* Survey	CP	AP	AP	AP	P			P
7. *Preference* Survey— Individuals	CP	AP	AP				P	P
8. *Preference* Survey Consensus (Dept., Grade Level, Students)	C	A	A	A			P	P

FIG. 15. Implementation sequence and participation

as well as the schedule of days when various kinds of sampling will occur), and various checkpoints or scheduled times when reviews of progress should occur. Once this plan has been developed and approved, the training of the staff and possibly the advisory committee can begin (if this was not done as a preliminary step).

The media staff and/or the individuals responsible for carrying out the various planning activities, such as collecting data or conducting group priority-determination sessions, will obviously need orientation and training to carry out these functions. This can be organized as an in-service training activity for media staff, for example, and can be directed by the

	MEDIA STAFF	PRINCIPAL	ADVISORY COM- MITTEE	STUDENT COUNCIL	TEACHERS	STUDENTS	TEACHER SAMPLE	STUDENT SAMPLE
(continued)								
9. *Preference Consensus—* Overall	C	A					P (REP'S)	P (REP'S)
10. Present Results of *Inventory* Survey	C	A	A	P	P	P		
11. Complete *Matrix* and Program Analysis	C	A	A					
12. Present Priorities, Capability, Changes	C	A	A		P	P		
13. Implemen- tation of New Program	C							
14. Reevalua- tion and Program Revision	C	A	A	P			P	P

Key: C Conducts A Assists P Participates

media specialist who is responsible for the overall program or the individual who is most interested in and familiar with the process and techniques. The explanations and instructions presented here will be sufficient for many, whereas others may wish to prepare themselves prior to implementation, for example, by attending workshops that are offered to train individuals in the process and techniques.

Another approach, in which the writer has frequently been involved, is the use of a consultant to conduct a one- or two-day in-service workshop to provide the initial training of the staff in pilot programs as well as to assist in developing a detailed implementation plan. This approach has been particularly successful where appropriate administrative personnel (as well as selected teachers) have been involved with the media personnel in the in-service workshops and where there has been an opportunity for one or more follow-up visits or telelectures to resolve any problems.

Whatever approach is used, basic understanding of the planning process and techniques should obviously be accomplished, either prior to or during the early stages of implementation.

The orientation of the media staff, principal, and advisory committee can also be carried out as a small pilot test of planning steps 2 and 3 (see step 2 in figure 15). This approach will orient the participants to the planning activities, which involve client participation, and may also serve as a method of training these individuals to assist in administering the survey, as well as conducting the priority-determination sessions (if a number of these are planned). Giving these key individuals a sample experience with these two techniques tends to be considerably more effective than a simple explanation in capturing their interest and cooperation. The perception and preference data derived from this small group may also be usable, at least in terms of indicating some areas of confusion regarding services, and may give some indication of service preferences and priorities to consider in program decision making even at this stage.

The media staff has the major responsibility and greatest time involvement in most of the implementation steps. However, the advisory committee and the principal can provide direct assistance in a number of implementation activities (see figure 15)—and can and possibly *should* be involved (to some degree) in analysis of the program when all the data have been collected (see steps 10, 11, and 12 in figure 15)—and participate in the presentation of the results. This assistance and real involvement of at least key individuals in planning and communicating the media program may very well make the major difference in terms of client response to the program and the degree to which resources are provided for the program.

The advisory committee may evolve into a continuing vehicle for client input to media program planning and evaluation. At the conclusion of the initial implementation of the process, an assessment should be made in terms of what further data should be collected in problem areas and for the continuous analysis and reporting of program achievements (outputs) and resource utilization, as well as operational performance. The advisory committee can play an important role here, as well as in providing additional inputs for the various and continuing reporting activities (for example, annual reports) which should be carried on, whether required or not, in order to maintain effective communication with administrators and clients regarding media program achievements and needs and justifications for resource requests.

As illustrated, the implementation of this planning process and the utilization of the various techniques can occur in different ways, on different scales, at different rates, and even in separate applications of a partial selection of the techniques incorporated in the overall process. The time required to accomplish the various activities will depend on all these factors, as well as on the specific organization and arrangements of a given media program and the capability of the media staff. Time estimates have been given where possible, and particularly in instances where individuals other than the media staff are involved.

In the writer's experience, individual implementation plans can vary from what could be described as delusions of grandeur to those which could be considered extremely timid. In the first case, the plan is almost doomed to failure because of an unrealistic scale and inadequate consideration of the time and effort required. In the second case, the ultimate benefits of the application of the process are usually not realized because the process was applied in only a very partial manner or with so modest an effort that there is little confidence in the results or little feedback and reinforcement from the communication and client interaction efforts.

Obviously, some locally appropriate middle ground is desirable and should be carefully calculated. A beginning, however, is essential, and some frustrations and misjudgments are to be expected in an endeavor as complex as planning, managing, and communicating media programs. It is time that we begin to recognize more clearly the complex and changing nature of the program management and development tasks we face and prepare ourselves to respond with more appropriate and effective management means. The process and techniques suggested here are offered to provide concrete assistance to media personnel in fashioning more systematic and assertive planning and communicating behavior.

Concluding Comments

The current degree and extent of use of this particular planning process have not been systematically or comprehensively surveyed since funds to accomplish this have not been available to this point. From the feedback received through involvement in introducing the process, as well as from feedback volunteered from individuals who are using the process in numerous parts of the country, implementation appears to be occurring more rapidly and widely than would be expected. The only "promotion" up to this point has been a few preliminary publications and the presentations of the writer, which are described in the preface. The demands for training sessions, which have far exceeded the time available, and the extent of early use, are encouraging to say the least and seem to indicate a real desire for concrete techniques in this area.

General awareness of inadequacies in planning and managing approaches and readiness to at least consider newer approaches seem to be increasing rapidly. The best description of current use of this specific process, however, would classify it in the early adoption stage in the rather common continuum for the dissemination of innovations: early adopters, middle adopters, and late adopters. In many cases early adoption was stimulated by the leadership of state and district media supervisors who organized in-service training programs and pilot programs. It is interesting to note, however, that in many cases where implementation was the most thorough and comprehensive, it was essentially due to the individual efforts of a single media specialist's exercising his initiative.

An effort to document examples of implementation in a series of case studies is under way. It is hoped that a good selection of cases can be identified and included in a publication of case studies of the implementation of program planning and evaluation. The demand for such information is constant and the value of thoroughly documented case studies of the implementation of the process would be of considerable assistance to others who are just beginning or considering implementation.

Any reliable norms or performance measures are totally lacking for comparison purposes to help assess a given program's use of resources, operational efficiency, or service output levels in relation to specific kinds of instructional program or learner characteristics. As more programs collect and report the kind of data suggested here, or as states or districts develop uniform reporting procedures which require this kind of data, it may be possible to begin to develop at least rough performance measures as guides. Some of the accountability systems are demanding this kind of data now, but we are not even close to having it available at this point. The possibility exists, however, that we may be able to develop some guides to the relationships between specific service outputs and a specific instructional program and learner needs, as well as between the specific numbers and kinds of resources needed to deliver specific kinds and levels of service outputs. To achieve this, a major effort must be mobilized to collect and analyze this kind of data from a good-size sample of media programs.

Experience thus far with the process clearly indicates that even though media specialists may not perceive it, they generally have considerable flexibility and potential control over how they use the most expensive and valuable resource in the program, staff time. The potential for increased efficiency and effectiveness in this area is frequently substantial, and even in the early stages of collecting time data significant changes to improve efficiency are usually identified and implemented. However, the serious problem of the lack of flexibility in reallocating funds among budget categories (for example, materials and staff) to meet the needs or service priorities of a specific school program will persist as long as strict formulas are adhered to for the allocation of materials, staff, and so forth. Ability to alter these allocation formulas to tolerate a different mix of services in different schools must be achieved before services can, in reality, be tailored to meet the individual needs of students and teachers in a given school. The hyprocrisy of talking of strict formula budgeting in the same breath with individualization seems to have escaped us.

The need for media specialists to assert—or rather insert—themselves in the budgetary planning process, rather than wait to be asked, is also readily apparent. Administrators have been found, more often than not, to be extremely receptive and responsive to representations from the media specialist when they are expressed and documented in the terms and format suggested here. The program planning and budgeting systems that are being developed in so many systems very frequently are totally instructional program oriented and do not reflect or accommodate the particular problems and characteristics of special program areas, such as media programs. Unless one is aware of this and is in a position to demonstrate these problems and make suggestions, the systems that are developed and adopted may very well create incredibly extensive documentation tasks which do not eventuate in an effective representation or justification of media program contributions and resource needs.

The planning process described here represents a combination of systematic management techniques, political techniques, and the application of professional judgment and expertise. The emphasis is on providing techniques to help the media specialist assert leadership and initiative in local program decision making. The bias is in favor of considerable local (building-level) and participatory decision making versus the centralization of decision making, which has been inadvertently fostered in some cases by the use of systematic management systems such as PPBS. The considerable and specifically documented client participation and input represents a check or counterinfluence on autonomous or unilateral administrative decision making which may not adequately reflect local or special program needs.

The perception that is characteristic of some media specialists, of a very passive rather than an active or assertive role as being most appropriate, may represent the most serious obstacle to implementation of this process.

The time required, the initial lack of familiarity with these kinds of techniques, and the misconception that current informal and intuitive methods will continue to be satisfactory also tend to reinforce any passive inclination and to provide rationalizations for not becoming familiar with and using such techniques. It would be naive to expect all media specialists to individually initiate the implementation of this process. Those in leadership positions and other, naturally innovative individuals are providing the examples and initiative.

The realization seems to be apparent, among some individuals, that the choice is clear-cut: manage or be managed—plan or accept the planning done by others—communicate the meaning of media programs to clients and administrators or accept poor use, confused client perceptions of the program, arbitrary and unexpected budget cuts, and teachers' negotiating for scheduled classes in the media center to provide them with planning time.

This work attempts to provide the technical and conceptual means for improvement in the planning and communicating of media programs. Hopefully, the means will be widely used and the ends of fostering learning and instruction will be served. Any technique or process can be used, or abused, depending on the intentions of the individual using it; but at least the potential is available to translate planning rhetoric into effective program behavior and service achievements.

APPENDIXES

Planning Instruments
for School Library
Media Programs

APPENDIX A

INVENTORY OF SCHOOL
LIBRARY/MEDIA CENTER SERVICES

1. Please identify (check x) yourself as to: Student _____, Teacher _____, Administrator _____, School Library/Media Specialist _____, Other (specify) _____.

2. Please use *pencil* so that you can easily change any answer.

3. Unless there are specific instructions to "SKIP" one or more questions, attempt to answer every question by checking (x) either "Yes" or "No." There are no right or wrong answers. Your answers should only reflect your present understanding of the services currently provided by the media center.

4. A "Yes" answer should mean that the specific service is consistently and currently provided. If a service is provided from time to time but is not provided regularly on demand, you may indicate this by writing in the word "Occasionally."

5. *Students* should answer only in terms of services provided for students and should ignore the teachers' column when separate columns are provided.

6. *Teachers, administrators,* and *media staff* should answer in terms of services provided both to teachers and students. Responses should be indicated in both the student and teacher columns when separate columns are provided. A "Yes" answer in the teacher column will be interpreted to mean the service is provided for all professional school staff.

Copyright © 1974 by James W. Liesener. Copies are available from Student Supply Store, University of Maryland, College Park, Md. 20742.

I. ACCESS TO MATERIALS, EQUIPMENT, AND SPACE

A. Provision of Materials

1. Does the media center provide the following materials (check only if answer is YES):	DIRECT ACCESS BY USER, SYSTEMATICALLY ORGANIZED ON SHELVES OR IN FILES	RESTRICTED ACCESS, STAFF DELIVERY ONLY
BOOKS		
Hardback	☐	☐
Paperback	☐	☐
Large print, talking, Braille (for the visually handicapped)	☐	☐
PERIODICALS		
General	☐	☐
Professional	☐	☐
NEWSPAPERS	☐	☐
PAMPHLET FILE MATERIALS	☐	☐
AUDIOVISUAL MATERIALS		
Art		
Framed reproductions	☐	☐
Objects	☐	☐
Prints (including study prints)	☐	☐
Audiotapes		
Cassette	☐	☐
Open reel	☐	☐
Charts	☐	☐
Displays	☐	☐
Films (silent and sound)		
8 mm. (regular and super 8)		
Cartridge	☐	☐
Reel-to-reel	☐	☐
16 mm.	☐	☐
Filmstrips (silent and sound)	☐	☐
Games	☐	☐
Maps and/or globes	☐	☐
Microforms (microfilm and microfiche)	☐	☐
Models	☐	☐
Mounted pictures	☐	☐
Multimedia kits	☐	☐
Phono records	☐	☐

	DIRECT ACCESS BY USER, SYSTEMATICALLY ORGANIZED ON SHELVES OR IN FILES	RESTRICTED ACCESS, STAFF DELIVERY ONLY
Photographs	☐	☐
Puzzles	☐	☐
Slides	☐	☐
Specimens	☐	☐
Transparencies	☐	☐
Videotapes		
Cassette	☐	☐
Reel-to-reel	☐	☐
Other (specify) _____		

B. Provision of AV Equipment

2. Does the media center provide the following types of AV equipment (check only if answer is YES):

	AVAILABLE TO STUDENTS	AVAILABLE TO TEACHERS
PROJECTORS		
8 mm. film (regular and super 8)	☐	☐
16 mm. film	☐	☐
Filmstrip	☐	☐
Slide	☐	☐
Overhead	☐	☐
Opaque	☐	☐
Micro	☐	☐
VIEWERS AND PREVIEWERS		
Filmstrip	☐	☐
Slide	☐	☐
PROJECTION SCREENS	☐	☐
RECORD PLAYERS	☐	☐
AUDIOTAPE RECORDERS AND PLAYERS		
Cassette	☐	☐
Reel-to-reel	☐	☐
VIDEOTAPE RECORDER AND PLAYBACK SYSTEMS		
(including related equipment)	☐	☐
RADIO RECEIVERS (AM/FM)	☐	☐

	AVAILABLE TO STUDENTS	AVAILABLE TO TEACHERS
TELEVISION		
Receivers/monitors	☐	☐
Closed-circuit system	☐	☐
Other (specify) _____		
CAMERAS		
Still picture	☐	☐
Motion picture	☐	☐
DELIVERY AND OTHER ASSOCIATED EQUIPMENT		
(e.g. carts, cords, microphones, tripods)	☐	☐
MICROFORM READERS	☐	☐
MICROFORM READER-PRINTERS	☐	☐
AUTOMATED LEARNING AND INFORMATION RETRIEVAL SYSTEMS		
Talking typewriters	☐	☐
Dial-access information retrieval systems (DAIRS)	☐	☐
Instructional response system consoles (ISRS)	☐	☐
Other (specify) _____		

C. Provision of Space

	YES	NO
3. Is space provided for individuals		
To read or study at tables	☐	☐
At individual carrels	☐	☐
To use nonprint media and necessary equipment	☐	☐
4. Is space provided for group use of the media center		
In separate conference rooms	☐	☐
In special area in media center	☐	☐
5. Does the media center provide individual carrels that are wired and fully equipped for a variety of electrical instructional media?	☐	☐
6. Does the media center provide space for special collections (e.g. reserve or classroom projects)?	☐	☐
7. Is space provided in the media center where users can leave materials for later use (e.g. lockers)?	☐	☐

D. Use of Materials, Equipment, and Space

USE OF THE MEDIA CENTER

8. When can the media center be used

	STUDENTS	TEACHERS
Before school	☐	☐
During school	☐	☐
After school	☐	☐
Week nights	☐	☐
Weekends	☐	☐
Vacations	☐	☐
Summer	☐	☐

	YES	NO
9. May students use the media center at any time as the need arises in the classroom?	☐	☐
10. Do students need their teacher's permission to go to the media center?	☐	☐
11. May small groups (4 or 5 students) be sent to the media center with assignments that require help from the media specialist?	☐	☐
If NO, skip to question 12. If YES, must teachers make arrangements with the media specialist in advance for this service?	☐	☐
12. May parents borrow materials from the media center?	☐	☐
13. May individuals not connected with the school Use the media center?	☐	☐
Check out materials?	☐	☐
14. Are policies and procedures for use of the media center developed *cooperatively* by the principal, teachers, students, and media specialists?	☐	☐

CIRCULATION OF MATERIALS AND EQUIPMENT

Check-out Procedures

15. May users check out materials and equipment for use in the classroom and outside the school as well as in the media center?
    (Check only if answer is YES):

	IN MEDIA CENTER ONLY		IN CLASSROOM		OUTSIDE SCHOOL	
	STUDENTS	TEACHERS	STUDENTS	TEACHERS	STUDENTS	TEACHERS
Books	☐	☐	☐	☐	☐	☐
Newspapers	☐	☐	☐	☐	☐	☐
Pamphlet file materials	☐	☐	☐	☐	☐	☐
Periodicals						
Current	☐	☐	☐	☐	☐	☐
Back issues	☐	☐	☐	☐	☐	☐
AV materials	☐	☐	☐	☐	☐	☐
AV equipment	☐	☐	☐	☐	☐	☐
Production materials	☐	☐	☐	☐	☐	☐

Borrowing Limitations

16. Is there a limit on the number of books, periodicals, and nonprint materials that users can take out at one time?

	AVAILABLE TO			
	STUDENTS		TEACHERS	
	YES	NO	YES	NO
Books	☐	☐	☐	☐
Periodicals	☐	☐	☐	☐
Nonprint materials	☐	☐	☐	☐

If YES, please indicate limitation

_____

17. Does the media center allow long-term loans (e.g. over vacation periods or during the summer)?   ☐   ☐   ☐   ☐

Renewals

18. May users renew books, periodicals, nonprint materials, and equipment?

Books	☐	☐	☐	☐
Periodicals	☐	☐	☐	☐
Nonprint materials	☐	☐	☐	☐
Equipment	☐	☐	☐	☐

Overdue Items

19. Does the media center promptly issue notices to users when items are overdue?   ☐   ☐   ☐   ☐

20. Are there fines for overdue items?   ☐   ☐   ☐   ☐

	AVAILABLE TO			
	STUDENTS		TEACHERS	
	YES	NO	YES	NO
21. If an item is overdue and not returned, are users allowed to take out another?	☐	☐	☐	☐

Recall

22. If someone wants an item that a user has checked out, will the media specialist ask to have it returned before it is due?	☐	☐	☐	☐
If NO, skip to question 23.				
If YES, is original user allowed to keep materials for a specified period before such recall notice is issued?	☐	☐	☐	☐
If YES, is user holding material penalized if he does not return the recalled material promptly?	☐	☐	☐	☐
23. When users are not in the media center, may they ask for materials by sending a note or another person?	☐	☐	☐	☐

STUDENTS, DO NOT
ANSWER 24, SKIP TO 25.

24. May a teacher request that a special collection be sent to her classroom for use there?			☐	☐

Reservation

25. May users ask that materials that are in the media center be held for them until they get there?	☐	☐	☐	☐
26. May users ask that materials that are out of the media center be reserved for them when returned?	☐	☐	☐	☐
If YES, is the material automatically sent to the user?	☐	☐	☐	☐
If NO, is the user notified?	☐	☐	☐	☐
27. If the requested material will take considerably longer to obtain than originally estimated, is the user notified of this fact?	☐	☐	☐	☐

STUDENTS, DO NOT
ANSWER 28–30, SKIP TO 31.

FORSYTH LIBRARY
FORT HAYS KANSAS STATE COLLEGE

	AVAILABLE TO			
	STUDENTS		TEACHERS	
	YES	NO	YES	NO
28. Does the media center provide a reserve shelf for classes working on a special topic if the teacher requests it?			☐	☐
29. Does the media center provide a reserve collection for materials in heavy demand?			☐	☐
30. Does media center staff schedule use of equipment so that conflicts with plans of other teachers are avoided?			☐	☐
31. Are there regular procedures whereby individuals, small groups, and classes can reserve equipment and space for viewing and listening in the media center?	☐	☐	☐	☐

E. PROVISION OF MATERIALS NOT IN THE MEDIA CENTER COLLECTION

	STUDENTS		TEACHERS	
	YES	NO	YES	NO
32. When users cannot find materials they need in the media center, does the media specialist borrow them from other sources?	☐	☐	☐	☐
If NO, skip to question 33.				
If YES, will the media center obtain the material even if the user could obtain a copy from local sources?	☐	☐	☐	☐
If YES, does the media center's decision to obtain material depend upon				
Type of material	☐	☐	☐	☐
Subject of material	☐	☐	☐	☐
Cost of material	☐	☐	☐	☐
Source	☐	☐	☐	☐
If YES, when material has been obtained from outside sources, is the user allowed to take it out of the media center, provided that the lender does not specify otherwise?	☐	☐	☐	☐
If YES, does the user generally pay any of the charges for interlibrary loan?	☐	☐	☐	☐
33. Does the media center sell materials?	☐	☐	☐	☐
34. Does the media center order for the media center materials requested by the user?	☐	☐	☐	☐

STUDENTS, DO NOT
ANSWER 35–37, SKIP TO 38.

F. Special Collections

| | AVAILABLE TO | | | |
| | STUDENTS | | TEACHERS | |
	YES	NO	YES	NO

35. Does the media center collect and make available special collections geared to the needs of individual classes? | | | ☐ | ☐ |

    If NO, skip to question 36.

    If YES, are these collections made available

        In the media center? | | | ☐ | ☐ |

        In the classroom? | | | ☐ | ☐ |

36. Does the media center provide a professional collection for teachers? | | | ☐ | ☐ |

37. Does the media center provide a special collection for parents? | | | ☐ | ☐ |

G. Copying

38. Does the media center provide copy machines to make copies of materials? ☐ ☐ ☐ ☐

39. Are users permitted to use the copy machine by themselves? ☐ ☐ ☐ ☐

    If NO, will a media staff member make a copy for them? ☐ ☐ ☐ ☐

40. Do users have to pay for the use of the copy machine? ☐ ☐ ☐ ☐

41. Is there a limit on the number of pages that can be copied at one time by users? ☐ ☐ ☐ ☐

42. May something be copied for users if they are not in the library? ☐ ☐ ☐ ☐

II. REFERENCE SERVICES

A. Provision of Reference Materials for Self-Help

43. Does the media center provide the following reference materials (Check only where answer is YES):

| | FOR WHOM | | FOR USE IN | | |
	S	T	MEDIA CENTER	CLASS	OUTSIDE SCHOOL
Basic tools for self-help	☐	☐	☐	☐	☐

	FOR WHOM			FOR USE IN	
	S	T	MEDIA CENTER	CLASS	OUTSIDE SCHOOL

Encyclopedias
Other reference
   tools, e.g.
   dictionaries,
   almanacs   ☐ ☐   ☐   ☐   ☐

Comprehensive
   tools for
   self-help, e.g.
   subject indexes   ☐ ☐   ☐   ☐   ☐

B. Identification and Location of Materials in Media Center

	AVAILABLE TO			
	STUDENTS		TEACHERS	
	YES	NO	YES	NO
44. Does the media center provide assistance on request to identify and locate materials?	☐	☐	☐	☐
45. When user is not in the media center, may he telephone requests or send requests by messenger to locate and identify materials?	☐	☐	☐	☐

C. Identification and Location of Materials Not in Media Center

	STUDENTS		TEACHERS	
	YES	NO	YES	NO
46. Does the media center provide information regarding materials in collections other than the school media center (e.g. book catalogues of the public library, lists from special libraries)?	☐	☐	☐	☐
47. When users cannot find the materials they need in the media center, does the media specialist check other sources for the needed materials and *refer* users to these sources?	☐	☐	☐	☐
48. When users cannot find the materials they need in the media center, does the media specialist check other sources and *make arrangements* for users to get materials?	☐	☐	☐	☐
If NO, skip to question 49.				
If YES, are arrangements made				
For individuals	☐	☐	☐	☐
For groups	☐	☐	☐	☐
49. Does the media center maintain a file of community resources?	☐	☐	☐	☐

D. ALERTING THE USER AND CURRENT AWARENESS SERVICES

	AVAILABLE TO			
	STUDENTS		TEACHERS	
	YES	NO	YES	NO

50. Does the media center regularly inform users of new acquisitions? ☐ ☐ ☐ ☐

    If NO, skip to question 51.

    If YES, please check for whom and for what:

	STUDENTS		TEACHERS	
	YES	NO	YES	NO
Materials	☐	☐	☐	☐
Equipment	☐	☐	☐	☐
Services	☐	☐	☐	☐

    If YES, are users provided with the opportunity to identify relevant materials which the media center will send to them? ☐ ☐ ☐ ☐

51. Does the media center provide special programs or displays to publicize such events as book week, national library week, film awards, etc.?

YES	NO
☐	☐

    If NO, skip to question 52.

    If YES, does the media center staff plan and prepare assembly programs about use of the media center, of media, of information networks, or libraries, etc.? ☐ ☐

    If YES, does the media center staff plan and prepare bulletin boards, displays, exhibits in the school? ☐ ☐

52. Does the media center provide the school newspaper with releases on (please check appropriate answer):

    School media center activities for teachers and students ☐ ☐

    Public library activities for teachers and students ☐ ☐

    Reviews and/or annotations of materials ☐ ☐

    Film programs ☐ ☐

    Radio, TV, and other mass media programs ☐ ☐

53. Does the media center provide the local newspaper with releases on school media program activities? ☐ ☐

54. Does the media staff provide talks to parent groups on materials and services for children or young adults? ☐ ☐

55. Does the media staff give talks to youth groups and clubs on appropriate materials and services?

	YES	NO
	☐	☐

STUDENTS, DO NOT
ANSWER 56, SKIP TO 57.

56. Does the media center provide information on available in-service workshops, courses, educational meetings, and professional activities to teachers?

	YES	NO
	☐	☐

	AVAILABLE TO			
	STUDENTS		TEACHERS	
	YES	NO	YES	NO

57. Does the media center try to identify the information needs of its users?

Q57	☐	☐	☐	☐

If NO, skip to question 58.

If YES, does the media center assess user needs on an informal basis, e.g. through personal contact with users? ☐ ☐ ☐ ☐

If YES, does the media center assess user needs on a formal basis by recording interests and maintaining a file of users' interests? ☐ ☐ ☐ ☐

Does the media center *systematically* notify users about materials relevant to their identified interests? ☐ ☐ ☐ ☐

Are items of individual interest routed to users? ☐ ☐ ☐ ☐

E. Assistance in Compiling Bibliographies

58. If the user requests materials on a certain topic, will the media specialist *help* him to make up the list? ☐ ☐ ☐ ☐

59. Will the media specialist give the user a list? ☐ ☐ ☐ ☐

If NO, is the user directed to existing lists of citations? ☐ ☐ ☐ ☐

If NO, skip to question 60.

If YES, are "quick" subject searches made if the user indicates he will be satisfied with a sample list of citations? ☐ ☐ ☐ ☐

If YES, are exhaustive lists (i.e. as complete as possible, given the resources and bibliographic tools of your media center) also prepared as a regular service of the media center? ☐ ☐ ☐ ☐

If YES, do these lists include nonprint materials where possible? ☐ ☐ ☐ ☐

| | AVAILABLE TO | | | |
| | STUDENTS | | TEACHERS | |
	YES	NO	YES	NO

60. As a regular service, does the media center undertake to evaluate the quality of materials relevant to a given request, besides providing a selected list of references? □ □ □ □

61. Does the media center prepare annotations and/or critiques for users in screening long lists of references? □ □ □ □

62. Does the media center prepare bibliographies for subjects that appear regularly in the school curriculum (e.g. Shakespeare in English, Nematodes in biology, set theory in math)? □ □ □ □

63. Does the media center provide access to any computer searching services, e.g. ERIC? □ □ □ □

F. ANSWER SERVICES

64. Does the media specialist give users the answer to a simple fact question (e.g. who was the author of *Jane Eyre*)? □ □ □ □
    If NO, skip to question 65.
    If YES, does the media specialist provide direct answers to simple fact questions over the phone or through a student messenger? □ □ □ □

65. Does the media specialist provide users with direct answers to more complex questions? □ □ □ □
    If NO, skip to question 66.
    If YES, does the media specialist answer more complex questions by phone or through a student messenger? □ □ □ □

66. If a question is beyond the subject matter competence of the media specialist, does the media specialist refer users to a subject matter specialist (e.g. biology teacher)? □ □ □ □
    If NO, skip to question 67.
    If YES, are there formal arrangements for subject matter specialists to provide specialized service to the media center on a regular basis? □ □ □ □

III. PRODUCTION SERVICES

A. PROVISION OF MATERIALS FOR USE BY STUDENTS AND/OR TEACHERS

	AVAILABLE TO			
	STUDENTS		TEACHERS	
	YES	NO	YES	NO

67. Does the media center provide users with materials, equipment, and facilities (space, etc.) for production functions? ☐ ☐ ☐ ☐

    If NO, skip to question 68.

    If YES, please check the production functions:

        Graphics (coloring, lettering, mounting) ☐ ☐ ☐ ☐
        Reprography (Xerox, mimeo, ditto, etc.) ☐ ☐ ☐ ☐
        Photography ☐ ☐ ☐ ☐

        May photographic materials be used
            In class ☐ ☐ ☐ ☐
            Outside the building ☐ ☐ ☐ ☐

B. PROVISION OF ASSISTANCE IN PRODUCTION

68. Does the media center provide assistance in the production of materials or the adaptation of commercially produced materials in

    Graphics ☐ ☐ ☐ ☐
    Reprography ☐ ☐ ☐ ☐
    Photography ☐ ☐ ☐ ☐

C. PRODUCTION OF MATERIALS BY MEDIA CENTER STAFF FOR USERS

69. Does the media center staff produce instructional materials for the user? ☐ ☐ ☐ ☐

    If YES, skip to question 70.

    If NO, does the media center staff refer the user to a source which will produce materials for the user? ☐ ☐ ☐ ☐

    If NO, will the media center staff handle the referral and make arrangements to obtain the finished product for the user? ☐ ☐ ☐ ☐

    If NO, skip to question 71.

| | AVAILABLE TO | | | |
| | STUDENTS | | TEACHERS | |
	YES	NO	YES	NO

70. Which of the following services are provided (please check)

Mounting of materials ☐ ☐ ☐ ☐

Laminating of materials ☐ ☐ ☐ ☐

Preparation of stencils ☐ ☐ ☐ ☐

Graphic displays ☐ ☐ ☐ ☐

Preparation of slides and slide sets ☐ ☐ ☐ ☐

Production and preparation of photo prints ☐ ☐ ☐ ☐

Production of videotapes ☐ ☐ ☐ ☐

Preparation of media kits
Audiotapes ☐ ☐ ☐ ☐
Slides with tapes ☐ ☐ ☐ ☐
Pictures with tapes ☐ ☐ ☐ ☐
Films with tapes ☐ ☐ ☐ ☐

Editing
Tapes ☐ ☐ ☐ ☐
Films ☐ ☐ ☐ ☐
Slides ☐ ☐ ☐ ☐
Videotapes ☐ ☐ ☐ ☐

Preparing scripts and storybook presentations ☐ ☐ ☐ ☐

Writing study guides, booklets, brochures ☐ ☐ ☐ ☐

Information leaflets ☐ ☐ ☐ ☐

Puppet and marionette theaters ☐ ☐ ☐ ☐

Working models and mock-ups ☐ ☐ ☐ ☐

Other (specify) _____

_____

71. Are instructional television programs produced and distributed through one or more of the following arrangements (check only if YES)

Procurement of programs from external sources ☐   ☐

Off-the-air recording and playback ☐   ☐

Central studio production and transmission ☐   ☐

School-building production and transmission ☐   ☐

Other (specify) _____

_____

IV. INSTRUCTION

A. DIRECTIONAL SERVICES

	YES	NO
72. Does the media center provide pamphlets, maps, or slide/tape kits, etc., describing the arrangement of the media center?	☐	☐
73. Does the media center provide a handbook for users (or a section in a school handbook)?	☐	☐

B. FORMAL INSTRUCTION AND ORIENTATION PROGRAMS

74. Does the media center provide a formal orientation program? ☐ ☐

75. Does the media center provide opportunities for students to develop skills and knowledge through participation in the media program, e.g. media center clubs, student-assistant programs? ☐ ☐

76. Does the media center staff take responsibility for arranging trips to public libraries, special libraries, museums, etc., to increase knowledge of outside information resources? ☐ ☐

STUDENTS, DO NOT
ANSWER 77–80, SKIP TO 81.

77. Does the media center provide formal instruction (e.g. scheduled class sessions) in the use of resources? ☐ ☐

    If NO, skip to question 78.

    If YES, does this instruction include

	YES	NO
Identification, location, and organization of materials and information, including the card catalog, etc.	☐	☐
Reference materials and skills	☐	☐
Research skills	☐	☐
Audiovisual equipment use and handling	☐	☐
Use of automated learning systems	☐	☐
Production materials (graphics, photography, reprography)	☐	☐
Evaluation and use of print media	☐	☐
Evaluation and use of nonprint media	☐	☐

	YES	NO

78. Does the school media specialist, upon request, provide classroom presentations (i.e. go into the classroom as a resource person) on media center resources and services related to specific projects or needs?   ☐   ☐

C. IN-SERVICE TRAINING

79. Does the media center conduct and/or participate actively in in-service educational programs for

	YES	NO
Media staff	☐	☐
Teachers	☐	☐
Teacher aides	☐	☐
Student teachers	☐	☐

80. Do in-service programs for teachers, teacher aides, and student teachers develop proficiency in

	YES	NO
Production and use of materials	☐	☐
Use and handling of equipment	☐	☐
Selection and evaluation of media	☐	☐
Utilization of nonprint materials for classroom instruction	☐	☐
Utilization of print materials for classroom instruction	☐	☐
Use of automated learning and information retrieval systems	☐	☐

D. INFORMAL INSTRUCTION

81. Does the media center, upon request, offer individual users instruction regarding identification, location, and organization of materials and information, including the card catalog, etc.?   ☐   ☐

	YES	NO
Reference materials and skills	☐	☐
Research skills	☐	☐
Audiovisual equipment use and handling	☐	☐
Use of automated learning systems	☐	☐
Production materials (graphics, photography, reprography)	☐	☐
Evaluation and use of print media	☐	☐
Evaluation and use of nonprint media	☐	☐

E. Guidance in Reading, Viewing, and Listening

	YES	NO
82. Does the media center provide guidance activities in each of the following skills?		
Reading	☐	☐
Viewing	☐	☐
Listening	☐	☐
83. Does the media center provide *group* guidance in reading, viewing, and/or listening through		
Displays and exhibits	☐	☐
Distribution of lists of recommended materials on topics of interest	☐	☐
Formal instructional program	☐	☐
Discussions with class groups on request	☐	☐
Discussions regarding recreational or "free" reading, viewing, and listening with groups on request	☐	☐
84. Does the media center give *individual* guidance in reading, viewing, and/or listening through		
Assistance in selection of materials	☐	☐
Conferences with individuals	☐	☐
Individualized lists of materials	☐	☐
Conferences with teacher	☐	☐
Conferences with guidance counselor	☐	☐
Parent–teacher–media specialist conferences	☐	☐
Maintenance of interest files for students	☐	☐
Maintenance of reading, viewing, and listening records for individuals with periodic evaluation of progress	☐	☐
Other _____		

STUDENTS: You have completed the "Inventory." The remaining questions are for teachers and media staff only.

V. CONSULTING SERVICES

A. ADVISING INDIVIDUAL TEACHERS

	NO	YES, ON DEMAND ONLY	YES, ON A REGULAR BASIS
85. Does the media center provide consultation to individual teachers?			
On the selection of resources (e.g. textbooks, workbooks, audiovisual equipment) for teaching units	☐	☐	☐
On instructional materials for use by students to achieve instructional objectives	☐	☐	☐
On professional teaching and curriculum materials for use by the teacher in planning units	☐	☐	☐
On the design and evaluation of instructional strategies and content	☐	☐	☐

Other (specify) ＿＿＿＿＿＿＿＿＿＿

＿＿＿＿＿＿＿＿＿＿＿＿＿＿＿＿＿＿

＿＿＿＿＿＿＿＿＿＿＿＿＿＿＿＿＿＿

	YES	NO
86. Does the media center staff act as one of the channels of information to teachers regarding student progress?	☐	☐

B. ADVISING TEACHING TEAMS AND DEPARTMENT OR GRADE-LEVEL GROUPS

	NO	YES, ON DEMAND ONLY	YES, ON A REGULAR BASIS
87. Does the media center provide consultation to teaching teams and department or grade-level groups?			
On the selection of resources (e.g. textbooks, workbooks, audiovisual equipment) for teaching units	☐	☐	☐
On instructional materials for use by students to achieve instructional objectives	☐	☐	☐
On professional teaching and curriculum materials for use by the teacher in planning units	☐	☐	☐

	NO	YES, ON DEMAND ONLY	YES, ON A REGULAR BASIS
On the design and evaluation of instructional strategies and content	☐	☐	☐

Other (specify) _____

_____

_____

C. Overall Curriculum Planning

	YES	NO
88. Does the media center provide consultation to school and/or system curriculum committees on overall curriculum planning?	☐	☐

If NO, skip to question 89.

If YES, in which of the following ways is consultation provided

	YES	NO
Media center staff is represented on school curriculum committees.	☐	☐
Media center staff is not represented but works with committees	☐	☐
Media center staff is represented on system-level curriculum committees	☐	☐

D. Media Clearinghouse

	YES	NO
89. Does the media center serve as a clearinghouse (information, sample materials, and evaluation assistance) for textbooks and other learning materials?	☐	☐

APPENDIX B

FORM FOR DETERMINING PREFERENCES
FOR SCHOOL LIBRARY/MEDIA CENTER SERVICES

We are asking you to help decide which services that the media center provides are most important. You are going to assign points according to your idea of the importance of these services. There may be some services which are of no value to you; these services should receive a "0" score.

Follow these steps in assigning points:

Step 1. You are being asked to participate in establishing service priorities for the media center. Allocate 1,000 points among the broad categories (I–V) of service in such a way as to reflect your own opinion on the relative importance or value of these service categories.

Enter the number you assign to each of the numbered sections in the blank at the beginning of each section. The five numbers should total to 1,000. Please use a pencil so that you can revise the numbers if you change your mind.

Step 2. Divide the number given to each roman numeral section among the capital letter subsections. Enter the number for each subsection on the line by the capital letter. If a subsection is not worth any points, enter a "0."

Step 3. Follow the same procedure in breaking down the points allocated to the arabic numeral and small letter subsections. Be careful that the points assigned to each subsection add up to the points assigned to the points allocated to the whole section.

Step 4. As you go through the above steps, feel free to change your mind about the assignment of numbers. As you work with the more specific services, you may decide that a certain section needs more points and you will need to subtract points from another section in order to accomplish this change.

Copyright © 1974 by James W. Liesener. Copies are available from Student Supply Store, University of Maryland, College Park, Md. 20742.
NOTE: If you are not clear regarding what a specific service means, see the same section in the "Inventory of School Library/Media Center Services."

_____   I. ACCESS TO MATERIALS, EQUIPMENT, SPACE

_____   A. Provision of Materials

_____   1. Books
_____   2. Periodicals, newspapers, pamphlet materials
_____   3. Sound media (e.g. recordings, tapes)
_____   4. Visual media (e.g. films, filmstrips, slides, maps, art)
_____   5. Others (e.g. kits, games, models, puzzles, globes)

_____   B. Provision of AV Equipment

_____   1. Equipment for sound media (e.g. tape recorders and players, radios)
_____   2. Equipment for visual media (e.g. projectors, cameras, screens, readers)
_____   3. Television (e.g. receivers, monitors, cameras)
_____   4. Equipment for automated learning and information retrieval systems

_____   C. Provision of Space in Media Center
_____   1. Space to work (individually and in groups)
_____   2. Space to use audiovisual and electronic equipment (individually and in groups)
_____   3. Space for special collections (reserve or class projects)

_____   D. Use of Materials, Equipment, Space

_____   1. Use of media center (media center available for use)
_____   a. Available for use during school hours for individuals and groups
_____   b. Available for use evenings and weekends
_____   c. Available for use during vacations and summers

_____ d. Available to parents
and nonschool persons
_____ 2. Circulation services for materials and
equipment
_____ a. Provision for use of
materials and equipment
in media center and
school (including use of
materials outside the
school)
_____ b. Provision for use of
equipment outside the
school
_____ c. Provision of additional
circulation services such
as borrowing limitations,
renewals, recall, and
reservation

_____ E. Provision of Materials Not in Media Center
Collection

_____ 1. Provision of materials from other
sources outside the school
(e.g. interlibrary loans)
_____ 2. Purchasing materials for the media
center requested by users for
specialized needs
_____ 3. Sale of materials

_____ F. Provision of Special Collections

_____ 1. Provision of materials on special
subject on request
_____ 2. Provision of professional library for
teachers

_____ G. Provision of Copying Services for Users

_____   II. REFERENCE SERVICES

    _____   A. Provision of Collection of Reference Materials for Self-Help

    _____   B. Assistance in Identification and Location of Materials in Media Center

    _____   C. Assistance in Identification and Location of Materials outside the Media Center Collection (e.g. information about other collections and referral to other sources)

    _____   D. Alerting the User and Current Awareness Services

        _____   1. Notifying the users of new materials, equipment, and services on a regular basis

        _____   2. Providing programs and presentations which publicize special events, materials, services, etc.

        _____   3. Systematically gathering information about user interests and needs, and routing relevant information and materials regarding those interests and needs:

            _____   a. For teachers

            _____   b. For students

    _____   E. Assistance in Compiling Bibliographies

        _____   1. Assistance in preparing lists of references on a given subject

        _____   2. Provision of lists of references on a given subject *for* users on request

        _____   3. Provision of evaluative information in addition to references

        _____   4. Provision of access to and assistance in using computer searching services

    _____   F. Answer Services

        _____   1. Provision of answers to simple questions for users on request

_____ 2. Provision of answers to complex
questions on request, including the use
of subject matter specialists
(e.g. biology teacher) when necessary

_____ III. PRODUCTION SERVICES

_____ A. Provision of Materials, Equipment, and Facilities
for Users to Produce Instructional Materials
(including graphics, photography, and
reprography)

_____ B. Provision of Technical Assistance in Producing
Instructional Materials

_____ C. Production of Materials by Media Center Staff for
Users on Request (includes production of
instructional television programs)

_____ IV. INSTRUCTION

_____ A. Directional Services

_____ B. Provision of Formal Instruction and Orientation
Programs

_____ C. Provision of In-Service Training Programs

_____ D. Provision of Informal Instruction on Request

_____ E. Provision of Guidance in Reading, Viewing,
and Listening

_____ V. CONSULTING SERVICES

_____ A. Provision of Consultation to Individual Teachers
regarding Selection and Use of Instructional and
Professional Materials and Equipment and the
Design of Instructional Strategies and Content

_____   B. Provision of Consultation to Teaching Teams and
              Department or Grade-Level Groups

_____   C. Contributing to Overall Curriculum Planning in the
              School or System through Participation on
              Curriculum Planning Committees

_____   D. The Media Center Serves as a Clearinghouse
              for Instructional Media

APPENDIX C

SCHOOL LIBRARY/MEDIA PROGRAM
DATA COLLECTION GUIDE

This guide is to be used for collecting the data needed to complete the "School Library/Media Program Costing Matrix" and is composed of the following two parts:

Part I: Physical Resources and Services Data
Part II: Staff Time and Services Data

A careful review of the "School Library/Media Program Costing Matrix" with particular attention given to the accompanying footnotes should precede the use of this guide in collecting data.

Copyright © 1974 by James W. Liesener. Copies are available from Student Supply Store, University of Maryland, College Park, Md. 20742.

PART I: PHYSICAL RESOURCES AND SERVICES DATA

SERVICE I: ACCESS TO MATERIALS, EQUIPMENT, SPACE

PHYSICAL RESOURCE ELEMENTS BY SERVICE SUBDIVISIONS[1]	RESOURCE QUANTITIES				COSTS		SERVICE OUTPUTS	NUMBER OF UNFILLED REQUESTS
	CURRENT HOLDINGS	NUMBER ITEMS REPLACED	NUMBER ITEMS ADDED	TOTAL NO. ITEMS PURCHASED	COST RANGE	AVERAGE UNIT COST		
A. PROVISION OF MATERIALS								
Materials								
(Books)								
Hardback								
Paperback								
Large print, etc.								
(Periodicals)								
General								
Professional								
(Newspapers)								
(Pamphlet File Materials)								
(Audiovisual Materials)								
Art								
Framed reproductions								
Objects								
Prints								
Audio Tapes								
Cassette								
Open reel								

[1] If physical resources are used in other service subdivisions than those indicated here, they should be added with the service subdivision heading.

Charts																							
Displays																							
Films (silent and sound)																							
8 mm.																							
Cartridge																							
Reel-to-reel																							
16 mm.																							
Filmstrips (silent and sound)																							
Games																							
Maps and globes																							
Microforms																							
Models																							
Mounted pictures																							
Multimedia kits																							
Phono records																							
Photographs																							
Puzzles																							
Slides																							
Specimens																							
Transparencies																							
Videotapes																							
Cassette																							
Reel-to-reel																							
Other																							

SERVICE I: ACCESS TO MATERIALS, EQUIPMENT, SPACE

PHYSICAL RESOURCE ELEMENTS BY SERVICE SUBDIVISIONS	RESOURCE QUANTITIES				COSTS		SERVICE OUTPUTS	NUMBER OF UNFILLED REQUESTS
	CURRENT HOLDINGS	NUMBER ITEMS REPLACED	NUMBER ITEMS ADDED	TOTAL NO. ITEMS PURCHASED	COST RANGE	AVERAGE UNIT COST		
Supplies								
Index cards								
File folders								
Paper, bond								
B. PROVISION OF AV EQUIPMENT								
Equipment								
(Projectors)								
8 mm. film								
16 mm. film								
Filmstrip								
Slide								
Overhead								
Opaque								
Micro								
(Viewers and Previewers)								
Filmstrip								
Slide								

(Projection Screens)

(Record Players)

(Audiotape Recorders and Players)
  Cassette
  Reel-to-reel

(Videotape Recorder and Playback Systems)

(Radio Receivers)

(Television)
  Receivers/monitors
  Closed circuit
  Other

(Cameras)
  Still picture
  Motion picture

(Delivery and Other)

(Microform Readers)

(Microform Reader-Printers)

(Automated Learning and Information Retrieval Systems)

PHYSICAL RESOURCE ELEMENTS BY SERVICE SUBDIVISIONS	RESOURCE QUANTITIES				COSTS		SERVICE OUTPUTS	NUMBER OF UNFILLED REQUESTS
	CURRENT HOLDINGS	NUMBER ITEMS REPLACED	NUMBER ITEMS ADDED	TOTAL NO. ITEMS PURCHASED	COST RANGE	AVERAGE UNIT COST		
F. PROVISION OF SPECIAL COLLECTIONS								
Materials								
(Professional) Books								
Periodicals								
Other								
G. COPYING								
Materials and Supplies								
Paper								
Equipment								

SERVICE II: REFERENCE SERVICES

A. PROVISION OF REFERENCE
   COLLECTION

Materials
Encyclopedias
Basic tools
   (dictionaries, etc.)
Indexes

SERVICE III: PRODUCTION SERVICES

A. PROVISION OF MATERIALS,
   EQUIPMENT, AND FACILITIES
   FOR PRODUCTION

Materials and Supplies
Transparency materials
Construction paper
Audiotape

Film
35 mm. color

PHYSICAL RESOURCE ELEMENTS BY SERVICE SUBDIVISIONS[1]	RESOURCE QUANTITIES				COSTS		SERVICE OUTPUTS	NUMBER OF UNFILLED REQUESTS
	CURRENT HOLDINGS	NUMBER ITEMS REPLACED	NUMBER ITEMS ADDED	TOTAL NO. ITEMS PURCHASED	COST RANGE	AVERAGE UNIT COST		
A. PROVISION OF MATERIALS (cont.)								
Equipment								
Dry-mount press								
Lettering equipment								
Film editors								
8 mm.								
16 mm.								
C. PROVISION OF MATERIALS, EQUIPMENT, AND FACILITIES FOR USERS								
Materials and Equipment								

PART II: STAFF TIME AND SERVICES DATA

SERVICE I: ACCESS TO MATERIALS, EQUIPMENT, SPACE

SERVICE SUBDIVISIONS[1]	OPERATIONAL TASKS[2]	SAMPLE 1				SAMPLE 2, ETC.[4]	DAILY AVERAGE[5]	YEARLY AVERAGE[5]
		TIME[3]	SERVICE OUTPUTS	OPER-ATIONAL OUTPUTS[2]	UNFILLED REQUESTS			
A. PROVISION OF MATERIALS	Processing materials							
	Selection and evaluation (new and replacement items)							
	Maintenance of collection (inventory, reports, etc.)							

[1] For a more detailed delineation of service subdivisions, see the "Inventory of School Library/Media Center Services." If staff time is expended in other service subdivisions than those indicated here, the subdivision should be added and the time accounted for under it.

[2] Indicate only where the operational tasks and outputs are not identical with the service subdivision description or service output.

[3] Actual and/or estimated time spent in one day recorded in minutes and hours. Samples are to be staggered over time to achieve more accurate estimates. Sampling can be discontinued when figures display a consistent pattern and/or confidence of accuracy is achieved. Each staff member is to record his/her time on a separate form.

[4] Sufficient columns will have to be provided to accommodate number of sample days data are collected.

[5] From the samples collected the daily and yearly averages can easily be calculated for staff time, service and operational outputs, and unfilled requests. The average yearly staff time expended in each category should be expressed in terms of the percent of the total yearly time so that costs can later be calculated by multiplying by the appropriate salary.

SERVICE SUBDIVISIONS	OPERATIONAL TASKS	SAMPLE 1				SAMPLE 2, ETC.	DAILY AVERAGE	YEARLY AVERAGE
		TIME	SERVICE OUTPUTS	OPERATIONAL OUTPUTS	UNFILLED REQUESTS			
B. PROVISION OF AUDIO-VISUAL EQUIPMENT	Processing							
	Selection and evaluation							
	Maintenance and technical assistance							
C. PROVISION OF SPACE	General supervision of use of center							
D. USE OF MATERIALS, EQUIPMENT, SPACE	Circulation and scheduling tasks							
	Supervisory tasks							

E. PROVISION OF MATERIALS NOT IN COLLECTION

Developing use policies and procedures

Identifying, locating, etc.

F. PROVISION OF SPECIAL COLLECTIONS

Selection and organizing tasks

G. COPYING

Supervision of use, etc.

SERVICE II: REFERENCE SERVICES

SERVICE SUBDIVISIONS	OPERATIONAL TASKS	SAMPLE 1				SAMPLE 2, ETC.	DAILY AVERAGE	YEARLY AVERAGE
		TIME	SERVICE OUTPUTS	OPER- ATIONAL OUTPUTS	UNFILLED REQUESTS			
B. ASSISTANCE IN IDENTI- FYING AND LOCATING MATERIALS IN CENTER								
C. ASSISTANCE IN IDENTI- FYING AND LOCATING MATERIALS OUTSIDE CENTER								
D. ALERTING AND CURRENT AWARENESS SERVICES								
E. ASSISTANCE IN COMPILING BIBLIOGRAPHIES								
F. ANSWER SERVICES								

SERVICE III: PRODUCTION SERVICES

	Selection, order- ing, manage- ment, etc.		
A. PROVISION OF MATERIALS, EQUIPMENT, AND FACILITIES FOR PRODUCTION			

B. PROVISION OF ASSISTANCE IN PRODUCTION

C. PRODUCTION OF MATERIALS, EQUIPMENT, AND FACILITIES FOR USERS

- Design of transparencies
- Editing of tapes
- Preparing scripts

SERVICE IV: INSTRUCTION

A. DIRECTIONAL SERVICES

B. PROVISION OF FORMAL INSTRUCTION AND ORIENTATION

- Writing, editing, etc.

C. PROVISION OF IN-SERVICE TRAINING

D. PROVISION OF INFORMAL INSTRUCTION

E. GUIDANCE IN READING, VIEWING, AND LISTENING

- Assistance to groups
- Assistance to individuals

SERVICE V: CONSULTING SERVICES

SERVICE SUBDIVISIONS	OPERATIONAL TASKS	SAMPLE 1				SAMPLE 2, ETC.	DAILY AVERAGE	YEARLY AVERAGE
		TIME	SERVICE OUTPUTS	OPERATIONAL OUTPUTS	UNFILLED REQUESTS			
A. CONSULTATION TO INDIVIDUAL TEACHERS								
B. CONSULTATION TO TEACHING TEAMS, ETC.								
C. PARTICIPATION IN OVERALL CURRICULUM PLANNING								
D. PROVISION OF CLEARINGHOUSE FOR INSTRUCTIONAL MEDIA	Selection, evaluation, ordering, etc.							

APPENDIX D

SCHOOL LIBRARY/MEDIA PROGRAM
COSTING MATRIX

The following information regarding the school and the media staff and facilities should also be included with the Matrix to provide some description of the context of the program being analyzed.

_____ School level (grades)
_____ Number of students in school
_____ Number of teachers in school
_____ Number of professional librarians on media center staff*
_____ Number of media aides*
_____ Number of hours of student help
_____ Number of hours of volunteer help
_____ Number of square feet in media center
Description of audiovisual facilities ("wet" carrels, etc.)

_____
_____
_____

* Express in terms of full-time equivalents, e.g., .5 media aide (half-time aide).

Copyright © 1974 by James W. Liesener. Copies are available from Student Supply Store, University of Maryland, College Park, Md. 20742. Material here has been revised slightly for sake of format.

PROGRAM COSTING MATRIX[1]

SERVICE I: ACCESS TO MATERIALS, EQUIPMENT, SPACE

RESOURCE ELEMENTS BY SERVICE SUBDIVISIONS[2]	RESOURCE QUANTITIES				COSTS			SERVICE AND OPERATIONAL OUTPUTS[3]
	CURRENT HOLDINGS	ITEMS REPLACED	ITEMS ADDED	TOTAL ITEMS PURCHASED	COST RANGE	AVERAGE UNIT COST	PROGRAM (SERVICE) COST	
A. PROVISION OF MATERIALS								
Materials								
(Books)								
Hardback								
Paperback								
Large print, etc.								
(Periodicals)								
General								
Professional								
(Newspapers)								
(Pamphlet File Materials)								
(Audiovisual Materials)								
Art								
Framed reproductions								
Objects								
Prints								
Audiotapes								
Cassette								
Open reel								
Charts								
Displays								

Films (silent and sound)
8 mm.
Cartridge
Reel-to-reel
16 mm.
Filmstrips (silent and sound)
Games
Maps and globes
Microforms
Models
Mounted pictures
Multimedia kits
Phono records
Photographs
Puzzles
Slides
Specimens
Transparencies
Videotapes
Cassette
Reel-to-reel

[1] For detailed suggestions regarding the collection of data required to complete the matrix, see the "School Library/Media Program Data Collection Guide."

[2] For a detailed definition, see the "Inventory of School Library/Media Center Services."

[3] Service output equals the number of times an item or service is used or delivered. Operational output equals the number of times a particular operational task is performed. If unfilled request data are collected, they can be included in parentheses in the Service Output column immediately next to the appropriate service output figure.

RESOURCE ELEMENTS BY SERVICE SUBDIVISIONS	RESOURCE QUANTITIES					COSTS			SERVICE AND OPERATIONAL OUTPUTS
	CURRENT HOLDINGS	ITEMS REPLACED	ITEMS ADDED	TOTAL ITEMS PURCHASED	COST RANGE	AVERAGE UNIT COST	PROGRAM (SERVICE) COST		
A. PROVISION OF MATERIALS (cont.)									
Other									
Supplies[4]									
Index cards									
File folders									
Paper, bond									

[4] All supply costs for Service I: Access to Materials, Equipment, Space may be included here if further discrimination among the service subdivisions is unnecessary or impossible. Examples listed here are only for the purpose of illustrating how supplies are to be treated.

RESOURCE ELEMENTS BY SERVICE SUBDIVISIONS	RESOURCE QUANTITIES		COSTS		SERVICE AND OPERATIONAL OUTPUTS
	STAFF TIME				
	OPERATIONAL TASKS	AMOUNT OF TIME[5]	SALARY	PROGRAM (SERVICE) COSTS	
Staff	Processing materials				
	Selection and evaluation (new and replacement items)				
	Maintenance of collection (inventory, reports, etc.)				

[5] Each staff member's time should be included here separately and designated by a symbol so that salary differentials can be considered in calculating costs. Volunteer and unpaid student-assistant time should be indicated in number of hours but obviously no cost should be calculated.

Materials Costs _____

Supply Costs _____

Staff Costs ================

A. PROVISION OF MATERIALS COSTS

RESOURCE ELEMENTS BY SERVICE SUBDIVISIONS	RESOURCE QUANTITIES					COSTS			SERVICE AND OPERATIONAL OUTPUTS
	CURRENT HOLDINGS	ITEMS REPLACED	ITEMS ADDED	TOTAL ITEMS PURCHASED	COST RANGE	AVERAGE UNIT COST	PROGRAM (SERVICE) COST		
B. Provision of Audiovisual									
Equipment									
Equipment									
(Projectors)									
8 mm. film									
16 mm. film									
Filmstrip									
Slide									
Overhead									
Opaque									
Micro									
(Viewers and Previewers)									
Filmstrip									
Slide									
(Projection Screens)									
(Record Players)									

(Audiotape Recorders
  and Players)
  Cassette
  Reel-to-reel
(Videotape Recorder and
  Playback Systems)
(Radio Receivers)
(Television)
  Receivers/monitors
  Closed circuit
  Other. _____

(Cameras)
  Still picture
  Motion picture
(Delivery and Other)
(Microform Readers)
(Microform Reader-
  Printers)
(Automated Learning and
  Informational Retrieval
  Systems)

RESOURCE ELEMENTS BY SERVICE SUBDIVISIONS	RESOURCE QUANTITIES		COSTS		SERVICE AND OPERATIONAL OUTPUTS
	STAFF TIME		SALARY	PROGRAM (SERVICE) COSTS	
	OPERATIONAL TASKS	AMOUNT OF TIME			
B. PROVISION OF AUDIOVISUAL EQUIPMENT (cont.) *Staff*	Processing[6]				
	Selection and evaluation[7]				
	Maintenance and technical assistance[8]				

Equipment Costs _____
Staff Costs _____

B. PROVISION OF EQUIPMENT COSTS

C. PROVISION OF SPACE[9] *Staff*	General Supervision of use of center				

C. PROVISION OF SPACE COSTS _____

[6] Acquiring equipment is frequently a system-level operating cost and, if so, should be considered as an overhead cost here and not included.
[7] Also frequently a system-level function, and if building-level costs are minimal they could be accounted for under Selection and Evaluation of Materials, Part B.
[8] Also frequently involves system-level costs (overhead) as well as building-level costs, which are to be included here if media staff time is expended on this task.

[9] Initial cost of facilities is considered as a capital cost and not included here. Maintenance (custodial services, heat, light, etc.) is an overhead cost

RESOURCE ELEMENTS BY SERVICE SUBDIVISIONS	RESOURCE QUANTITIES		COSTS		SERVICE AND OPERATIONAL OUTPUTS[10]
	STAFF TIME		SALARY	PROGRAM (SERVICE) COSTS	
	OPERATIONAL TASKS	AMOUNT OF TIME			
D. USE OF MATERIALS, EQUIPMENT, SPACE *Staff*					
	Circulation and scheduling tasks				
	Supervisory tasks				
	Developing use policies and procedures				
E. PROVISION OF MATERIALS NOT IN COLLECTION *Staff*	Identifying, locating, etc.				

[10] Both Service and Operational Output figures should be recorded where both occur in the same service subdivision. For example, under D. For Use of Materials, individual and group use figures should be indicated as well as the number of times the various operational tasks were performed. The service output figures should always be listed first, followed by the operational output figures.

D. USE OF MATERIALS, EQUIPMENT, SPACE COSTS

E. PROVISION OF MATERIALS NOT IN COLLECTION COSTS

RESOURCE ELEMENTS BY SERVICE SUBDIVISIONS	RESOURCE QUANTITIES				COSTS			SERVICE AND OPERATIONAL OUTPUTS
	CURRENT HOLDINGS	ITEMS REPLACED	ITEMS ADDED	TOTAL ITEMS PURCHASED	COST RANGE	AVERAGE UNIT COST	PROGRAM (SERVICE) COST	
F. PROVISION OF SPECIAL COLLECTIONS								
Materials								
(Professional)[11]								
Books								
Periodicals								
Other____								

RESOURCE ELEMENTS BY SERVICE SUBDIVISIONS	RESOURCE QUANTITIES		COSTS		SERVICE AND OPERATIONAL OUTPUTS
	STAFF TIME		SALARY	PROGRAM (SERVICE) COSTS	
	OPERATIONAL TASKS	AMOUNT OF TIME			
Staff					
	Selection and organizing tasks				

Materials Costs _____
Staff Costs _____
= F. PROVISION OF SPECIAL COLLECTIONS COSTS

[11] If these materials are restricted to use by the school staff and the costs are identifiable, place these costs here, otherwise include them with the other

RESOURCE ELEMENTS BY SERVICE SUBDIVISIONS	RESOURCE QUANTITIES				COSTS			
	CURRENT HOLDINGS	ITEMS REPLACED	ITEMS ADDED	TOTAL ITEMS PURCHASED	COST RANGE	AVERAGE UNIT COST	PROGRAM (SERVICE) COST	SERVICE AND OPERATIONAL OUTPUTS
G. COPYING								
Materials and Supplies								
Paper								
Equipment[12]								

RESOURCE ELEMENTS BY SERVICE SUBDIVISIONS	RESOURCE QUANTITIES		COSTS		
	STAFF TIME		SALARY	PROGRAM (SERVICE) COSTS	SERVICE AND OPERATIONAL OUTPUTS
	OPERATIONAL TASKS	AMOUNT OF TIME			
Staff					
Supervision of use, etc.					

Materials and Supplies Costs _____

Equipment Costs _____

Staff Costs _____

G. COPYING COSTS _____

[12] Initial equipment costs here and/or rental charges can also be considered capital and overhead costs and therefore not included. Relative cost and mechanism used, as well as budget category involved, may influence whether these costs should be included as operating costs.

	STAFF ONLY	TOTAL	PERCENT OF TOTAL COST[13]	VALUE IN PERCENT[14]
A. PROVISION OF MATERIALS COSTS				
B. PROVISION OF AUDIOVISUAL EQUIPMENT COSTS				
C. PROVISION OF SPACE COSTS				
D. USE OF MATERIALS, ETC., COSTS				
E. PROVISION OF MATERIALS NOT IN COLLECTION COSTS				
F. PROVISION OF SPECIAL COLLECTIONS COSTS				
G. COPYING COSTS				
I. ACCESS TO MATERIALS, EQUIPMENT, SPACE COSTS				

[13] The percent of the total media program should be calculated for all service subdivisions as well as for the total of Service I.

[14] The value should be taken from the consensus figures derived in the priority determination sessions with clients and recorded on the "Form for Determining Preferences for School Library/Media Center Services."

SERVICE II: REFERENCE SERVICES

RESOURCE ELEMENTS BY SERVICE SUBDIVISIONS	RESOURCE QUANTITIES				COSTS			SERVICE AND OPERATIONAL OUTPUTS
	CURRENT HOLDINGS	ITEMS REPLACED	ITEMS ADDED	TOTAL ITEMS PURCHASED	COST RANGE	AVERAGE UNIT COST	PROGRAM (SERVICE) COST	
A. PROVISION OF REFERENCE COLLECTION								
Materials[15]								
Encyclopedias								
Basic tools (dictionaries, etc.)								
Indexes								

A. PROVISION OF REFERENCE COLLECTION COSTS

[15] Only purchase costs are included here. The costs for processing and selection, etc., should be included under Service I: Access, Subdivision A, because of the difficulty in differentiating these costs for only reference materials.

RESOURCE ELEMENTS BY SERVICE SUBDIVISIONS	RESOURCE QUANTITIES		COSTS		SERVICE AND OPERATIONAL OUTPUTS
	STAFF TIME		SALARY	PROGRAM (SERVICE) COSTS	
	OPERATIONAL TASKS	AMOUNT OF TIME			
B. ASSISTANCE IN IDENTIFYING AND LOCATING MATERIALS IN CENTER *Staff*					
C. ASSISTANCE IN IDENTIFYING AND LOCATING MATERIALS OUTSIDE CENTER *Staff*					
D. ALERTING AND CURRENT AWARENESS SERVICES *Staff*					
E. ASSISTANCE IN COMPILING BIBLIOGRAPHIES *Staff*					
F. ANSWER SERVICES *Staff*					

[16] Operational tasks are not specified here because they are obvious from the title of the service subdivision.

	STAFF ONLY	TOTAL	PERCENT OF TOTAL COST	VALUE IN PERCENT
A. PROVISION OF REFERENCE COLLECTION COSTS				
B. ASSISTANCE IN IDENTIFYING AND LOCATING MATERIALS IN CENTER COSTS				
C. ASSISTANCE IN IDENTIFYING AND LOCATING MATERIALS OUTSIDE CENTER COSTS				
D. ALERTING AND CURRENT AWARENESS SERVICES COSTS				
E. ASSISTANCE IN COMPILING BIBLIOGRAPHIES COSTS				
F. ANSWER SERVICES COSTS				
II. REFERENCE SERVICES COSTS				

SERVICE III: PRODUCTION SERVICES

RESOURCE ELEMENTS BY SERVICE SUBDIVISIONS	RESOURCE QUANTITIES				COSTS			SERVICE AND OPERATIONAL OUTPUTS
	CURRENT HOLDINGS	ITEMS REPLACED	ITEMS ADDED	TOTAL ITEMS PURCHASED	COST RANGE	AVERAGE UNIT COST	PROGRAM (SERVICE) COST	
A. PROVISION OF MATERIALS, EQUIPMENT, AND FACILITIES FOR PRODUCTION								
Materials and Supplies[17]								
Transparency materials								
Construction paper								
Audiotape								
Film								
35 mm. color								
Equipment[17]								
Dry-mount press								
Lettering equipment								
Film editors								
8 mm.								
16 mm.								

[17] Examples listed here are for illustrative purposes only. Regarding equipment, see footnote on page 129.

	RESOURCE QUANTITIES		COSTS		
RESOURCE ELEMENTS BY SERVICE SUBDIVISIONS	STAFF TIME		SALARY	PROGRAM (SERVICE) COSTS	SERVICE AND OPERATIONAL OUTPUTS
	OPERATIONAL TASKS[16]	AMOUNT OF TIME			
Staff	Selection, ordering, management, etc.				

Materials and Supplies Costs _____

Equipment Costs _____

Staff Costs _____

A. PROVISION OF MATERIALS, EQUIPMENT, FACILITIES COSTS

B. PROVISION OF ASSISTANCE IN PRODUCTION

Staff

RESOURCE ELEMENTS BY SERVICE SUBDIVISIONS	RESOURCE QUANTITIES				COSTS			SERVICE AND OPERATIONAL OUTPUTS
	CURRENT HOLDINGS	ITEMS REPLACED	ITEMS ADDED	TOTAL ITEMS PURCHASED	COST RANGE	AVERAGE UNIT COST	PROGRAM (SERVICE) COST	
C. PRODUCTION OF MATERIALS, EQUIPMENT, AND FACILITIES FOR USERS[18]								
Materials and Equipment[18]								

18 If it is possible to distinguish the materials and equipment used in this service category from Subdivision A, this should be done. However, if this is not possible or reasonable, they can be included with the materials, etc., in Subdivision A.

RESOURCE ELEMENTS BY SERVICE SUBDIVISIONS	RESOURCE QUANTITIES		COSTS		SERVICE AND OPERATIONAL OUTPUTS
	STAFF TIME		SALARY	PROGRAM (SERVICE) COSTS	
	OPERATIONAL TASKS	AMOUNT OF TIME			
Staff	Design of transparencies				
	Editing of tapes				
	Preparing scripts				

Materials and Equipment Costs _____

Staff Costs _____

C. PRODUCTION OF MATERIALS, EQUIPMENT, AND FACILITIES FOR USERS COSTS _____

	STAFF ONLY	TOTAL	PERCENT OF TOTAL COST	VALUE IN PERCENT
A. PROVISION OF MATERIALS, EQUIPMENT, AND FACILITIES FOR PRODUCTION COSTS				
B. PROVISION OF ASSISTANCE IN PRODUCTION COSTS				
C. PRODUCTION OF MATERIALS, EQUIPMENT, AND FACILITIES FOR USERS COSTS				

III. PRODUCTION SERVICES COSTS

SERVICE IV: INSTRUCTION

RESOURCE ELEMENTS BY SERVICE SUBDIVISIONS	RESOURCE QUANTITIES		COSTS		SERVICE AND OPERATIONAL OUTPUTS
	STAFF TIME		SALARY	PROGRAM (SERVICE) COSTS	
	OPERATIONAL TASKS	AMOUNT OF TIME			
A. DIRECTIONAL SERVICES[19] *Staff*	Writing, editing, etc.				
B. PROVISION OF FORMAL INSTRUCTION AND ORIENTATION *Staff*					
C. PROVISION OF IN-SERVICE TRAINING *Staff*					

[19] The materials costs could also be included here if they are identifiable.

RESOURCE ELEMENTS BY SERVICE SUBDIVISIONS	RESOURCE QUANTITIES		COSTS		SERVICE AND OPERATIONAL OUTPUTS
	STAFF TIME		SALARY	PROGRAM (SERVICE) COSTS	
	OPERATIONAL TASKS	AMOUNT OF TIME			
D. PROVISION OF INFORMAL INSTRUCTION *Staff*					
E. GUIDANCE IN READING, VIEWING, AND LISTENING *Staff*					
Assistance to groups					
Assistance to individuals					

	STAFF ONLY	TOTAL	PERCENT OF TOTAL COST	VALUE IN PERCENT
A. DIRECTIONAL SERVICES COSTS				
B. PROVISION OF FORMAL INSTRUCTION AND ORIENTATION COSTS				
C. PROVISION OF IN-SERVICE TRAINING COSTS				
D. PROVISION OF INFORMAL INSTRUCTION COSTS				
E. GUIDANCE IN READING, VIEWING, AND LISTENING COSTS				
IV. INSTRUCTION COSTS				

SERVICE V: CONSULTING SERVICES

RESOURCE ELEMENTS BY SERVICE SUBDIVISIONS	RESOURCE QUANTITIES		COSTS		SERVICE AND OPERATIONAL OUTPUTS
	STAFF TIME		SALARY	PROGRAM (SERVICE) COSTS	
	OPERATIONAL TASKS	AMOUNT OF TIME			
A. CONSULTATION TO INDIVIDUAL TEACHERS *Staff*					
B. CONSULTATION TO TEACHING TEAMS, ETC. *Staff*					
C. PARTICIPATION IN OVERALL CURRICULUM PLANNING *Staff*					
D. PROVISION OF CLEARINGHOUSE FOR INSTRUCTIONAL MEDIA *Staff*	Selection, evaluation, ordering, etc.				

	STAFF ONLY	TOTAL	PERCENT OF TOTAL COST	VALUE IN PERCENT
A. Consultation to Individual Teachers Costs				
B. Consultation to Teaching Teams, etc., Costs				
C. Participation in Overall Curriculum Planning Costs				
D. Provision of Clearinghouse for Instructional Media Costs				
V. CONSULTING SERVICES COSTS				

TOTAL PROGRAM (SERVICE) COSTS

	STAFF ONLY	TOTAL	PERCENT OF TOTAL COST	VALUE IN PERCENT
I. ACCESS TO MATERIALS, EQUIPMENT, AND SPACE				
II. REFERENCE SERVICES				
III. PRODUCTION SERVICES				
IV. INSTRUCTION				
V. CONSULTING SERVICES				
TOTAL				

APPENDIX E:

SUGGESTIONS FOR IDENTIFYING INDIRECT COSTS

The purpose of this Appendix is to provide suggestions for identifying and calculating indirect (overhead and capital) costs for a media program. These costs are not normally considered in planning and operating building-level media programs. However, these costs are extremely important if the total direct and indirect costs of a district's media program are to be accurately portrayed. These costs are obviously also important in planning new facilities and renovating old ones, but it is primarily district staff who are concerned with these costs rather than building-level media personnel. First overhead costs are discussed because they are the most difficult to calculate in such a way as to relate them to building-level media programs and services and then capital costs are briefly identified. Some general suggestions regarding potential sources of information are also included.

OVERHEAD COSTS

Overhead generally refers to such fixed costs as space (rent or depreciation), janitorial maintenance, heat, light, telephone, insurance, and so forth. Although many supply items are often considered part of overhead, the approach here has been to treat supplies as operating costs.

In addition to these common overhead costs, a building-level media program must also consider the costs of the back-up support provided by the district in the form of selection and evaluation assistance, processing and acquisitions operations, production services, instruction, centralized supporting collections, administrative services, and so forth. These complete the cost picture for media programs and indicate the resources which would have to be provided at the individual school level in the absence of district supporting services.

INDIVIDUAL SCHOOL OVERHEAD COSTS

Common overhead costs such as rent or depreciation, heat, light, telephone, and janitorial maintenance can probably most easily be figured in the following manner on a "per square foot" basis:

(1) determine total number of square feet in the school;
(2) determine number of square feet for media center program;
(3) determine percent of school total;
(4) multiply percent times total cost for each of the overhead categories.

While this process gives only a gross estimate of common overhead costs, the cost representation is nevertheless useful in planning and budgeting media center programs and in portraying more accurately the proportion of the total school budget expended for the media program.

DISTRICT MEDIA SUPPORT SERVICES[1]

In the case of district media support services, the "user"' is an individual school media center and "output" is the number of service units provided by the district to each "user." An additional problem arises when the district media program performs its services directly to individuals rather than to media centers. This frequently occurs with film loans, production services, or in-service training. One possible way to get around these "direct user services" might be to include them as services to a particular media program even though the service was to an individual. The cost would at least be a reflection of the school program to which the individual belonged.

Services commonly provided from the district level include:

 I. Assistance in Providing Access to Materials and Equipment:
     selection and evaluation services,
     processing services,
     provision of materials and equipment from district collections,
     maintenance and technical assistance;
 II. Production Services (graphics, photography, reprography, television, and videotape programs and equipment);
 III. Instruction (in-service programs, orientation, and so forth);
 IV. Consulting (e.g. individual assistance, staff selection, coordination of cooperative activities, promotional activities, and planning services).

The cost of district support services for a given media program might be derived as a gross average cost for support services or as a unit cost for a given support service. One possible approach for calculating the gross average cost for a support service is as follows:

(1) determine the total cost of a given service at the district level (such as total cost for selection and evaluation or for processing, production, and so forth);

(2) divide by the number of schools in the district;

(3) possibly add a weighting factor to represent enrollment and/or type of school (elementary, junior, senior high);

(4) this would produce a gross estimate of the cost for a given district support service.

A possible approach for calculating the unit cost for a given support service is as follows:

(1) determine the total cost of a given function at the district level;

(2) determine the output or use of the service: a quantitative number of services produced per year (such as number of materials selected and evaluated, number of transparencies made, number of materials processed);

---

[1] For a detailed description of district programs, see James W. Liesener, *District and Regional Learning Resource (Media) Programs: A Systematic Planning Process and Exploratory Survey of Services* (Texas Education Agency, 1975).

(3) divide the total cost of given service by the output;

(4) this would provide an average unit cost for a given service;

(5) determine the output or use associated with an individual media center;

(6) multiply the average unit cost by the output or use for a given media center to arrive at the cost of a specific district support service for a given media program.

In order to acquire the data necessary to calculate these costs, it is suggested that records similar to those recommended for individual media centers be kept for district costs, output, and use. This information might be found in some of the following sources:

(1) salary schedules;

(2) district budget requests and reports of operating expenditures for a given fiscal year. This would include the cost of staff, materials, equipment, and supplies for various services (such as selection and evaluation, processing);

(3) circulation, attendance, and use statistics for district library or curriculum laboratory or materials laboratory;

(4) circulation, output, use statistics for film library;

(5) reports of output from production department;

(6) average costs of books and nonprint materials from bids, invoices, and so forth;

(7) maintenance contracts on equipment;

(8) equipment bidding lists and purchase orders.

Overhead costs for such things as school or school district administration are not dealt with here and will have to be calculated according to local system procedures. This is one of a number of overhead items which ideally should be able to be broken down to reflect specific contributions to certain program outputs such as media services. However, attempting to make these kinds of discriminations becomes extremely arbitrary and ludicrous and it would seem to make much better sense to simply specify certain cost items as overhead without attempting to relate these to specific program outputs.

CAPITAL COSTS

Capital costs refer to the costs of initially establishing a media program. These include initial expenditures for construction of facilities, property, furnishings, equipment, materials, and supplies.[2] These costs are usually readily available in budget requests for capital expenditures and school district planning documents.

---

[2] Initial collections and so forth may not actually be provided out of capital budgets but usually funds are at least separately provided in district operating budgets for initial collections, for example, so that these costs can be considered in the same way as capital costs.

The suggestions made in this Appendix represent only a rough beginning at identifying and specifying the overhead and capital costs for media programs. It is clearly recognized that considerable additional work is required before these important cost categories can be adequately represented in the planning and budgeting of media programs.

APPENDIX F:

ANSWER SHEET FOR "INVENTORY OF SCHOOL LIBRARY/MEDIA CENTER SERVICES" (APPENDIX A)

INSTRUCTIONS

A. Please use *pencil* so that you can easily change any answer, and place all responses on the answer sheet.

B. Please identify (check x) yourself as to: Student _____, Teacher _____, Administrator _____, School Library/Media Specialist _____, Other (specify) _____.

C. Unless there are specific instructions to "SKIP" one or more questions, attempt to answer every question by checking (x) either "Yes" or "No." There are no right or wrong answers. Your answers should only reflect your present understanding of the services currently provided by the media center.

D. A "Yes" answer should mean that the specific service is consistently and currently provided. If a service is provided from time to time but is not provided regularly on demand, you may indicate this by writing in the word "occasionally."

E. *Students* should answer only in terms of services provided for students and should ignore the teachers' column when separate columns are provided.

F. *Teachers, administrators,* and *media staff* should answer in terms of services provided both to teachers and students. Responses should be indicated in both the student and teacher columns when separate columns are provided. A "Yes" answer in the teacher column will be interpreted to mean the service is provided for all professional school staff.

G. Numbers on the answer sheet correspond to the question number on the "Inventory of School Library/Media Center Services." The small letters are given for each suggestion to help in identification where appropriate, even though these sub-questions are not so labeled on the "Inventory of School Library/Media Center Services."

ANSWER SHEET

1. Does the media center provide the following materials (check only if answer is YES):

	DIRECT ACCESS BY USER, SYSTEMATICALLY ORGANIZED ON SHELVES OR IN FILES	RESTRICTED ACCESS, STAFF DELIVERY ONLY
BOOKS		
Hardback	☐	☐
Paperback	☐	☐
Large print, talking, Braille (for the visually handicapped)	☐	☐
PERIODICALS		
General	☐	☐
Professional	☐	☐
NEWSPAPERS	☐	☐
PAMPHLET FILE MATERIALS	☐	☐
AUDIOVISUAL MATERIALS		
Art		
Framed reproductions	☐	☐
Objects	☐	☐
Prints (including study prints)	☐	☐
Audiotapes		
Cassette	☐	☐
Open reel	☐	☐
Charts	☐	☐
Displays	☐	☐
Films (silent and sound)		
8 mm. (regular and super 8)		
Cartridge	☐	☐
Reel-to-reel	☐	☐
16 mm.	☐	☐
Filmstrips (silent and sound)	☐	☐
Games	☐	☐
Maps and/or globes	☐	☐
Microforms (microfilm and microfiche)	☐	☐
Models	☐	☐
Mounted pictures	☐	☐
Multimedia kits	☐	☐
Phono records	☐	☐

	DIRECT ACCESS BY USER, SYSTEMATICALLY ORGANIZED ON SHELVES OR IN FILES	RESTRICTED ACCESS, STAFF DELIVERY ONLY
Photographs	☐	☐
Puzzles	☐	☐
Slides	☐	☐
Specimens	☐	☐
Transparencies	☐	☐
Videotapes		
Cassette	☐	☐
Reel-to-reel	☐	☐

Other (specify) _____

B. PROVISION OF AV EQUIPMENT

2. Does the media center provide the following types of AV equipment (check only if answer is YES):

	AVAILABLE TO STUDENTS	AVAILABLE TO TEACHER
PROJECTORS		
8 mm. film (regular and super 8)	☐	☐
16 mm. film	☐	☐
Filmstrip	☐	☐
Slide	☐	☐
Overhead	☐	☐
Opaque	☐	☐
Micro	☐	☐
VIEWERS AND PREVIEWERS		
Filmstrip	☐	☐
Slide	☐	☐
PROJECTION SCREENS	☐	☐
RECORD PLAYERS	☐	☐
AUDIOTAPE RECORDERS AND PLAYERS		
Cassette	☐	☐
Reel-to-reel	☐	☐
VIDEOTAPE RECORDER AND PLAYBACK SYSTEMS		
(including related equipment)	☐	☐
RADIO RECEIVERS (AM/FM)	☐	☐

	AVAILABLE TO STUDENTS	AVAILABLE TO TEACHERS
TELEVISION		
Receivers/monitors	☐	☐
Closed-circuit system	☐	☐
Other (specify) _____		
CAMERAS		
Still picture	☐	☐
Motion picture	☐	☐
DELIVERY AND OTHER ASSOCIATED EQUIPMENT		
(e.g. carts, cords, microphones, tripods)	☐	☐
MICROFORM READERS	☐	☐
MICROFORM READER-PRINTERS	☐	☐
AUTOMATED LEARNING AND INFORMATION RETRIEVAL SYSTEMS		
Talking typewriters	☐	☐
Dial-access information retrieval systems (DAIRS)	☐	☐
Instructional response system consoles (ISRS)	☐	☐
Other (specify) _____		

		YES	NO
3.	a.		
	b.		
	c.		
4.	a.		
	b.		
5.			
6.			
7.			

		STUDENTS	TEACHERS
8.	a.		
	b.		
	c.		
	d.		
	e.		
	f.		
	g.		

		YES	NO
9.			
10.			
11.	a.		
	b.		
12.			
13.	a.		
	b.		
14.			
15.	See page 163.		

		STUDENTS		TEACHERS	
		YES	NO	YES	NO
16.	a.				
	b.				
	c.				
17.					

		STUDENTS		TEACHERS	
		YES	NO	YES	NO
18.	a.				
	b.				
	c.				
	d.				
19.					
20.					
21.					
22.	a.				
	b.				
	c.				
23.					
24.					
25.					
26.	a.				
	b.				
	c.				
27.					
28.					
29.					
30.					
31.					
32.	a.				
	b.				
	c.				
	d.				
	e.				
	f.				
	g.				
	h.				
33.					
34.					
35.	a.				
	b.				
	c.				
36.					
37.					
38.					

		STUDENTS		TEACHERS	
		YES	NO	YES	NO
39.	a.				
	b.				
40.					
41.					
42.					
43.		See page 163.			
44.					
45.					
46.					
47.					
48.	a.				
	b.				
	c.				
49.					
50.	a.				
	b.				
	c.				
	d.				
	e.				

		YES	NO
51.	a.		
	b.		
	c.		
52.	a.		
	b.		
	c.		
	d.		
	e.		
53.			
54.			
55.			
56.			

		STUDENTS		TEACHERS	
		YES	NO	YES	NO
57.	a.				
	b.				

		STUDENTS		TEACHERS					STUDENTS		TEACHERS	
		YES	NO	YES	NO				YES	NO	YES	NO
	c.						i.					
	d.						j.					
	e.						k.					
58.							l.					
59.	a.						m.					
	b.						n.					
	c.						o.					
	d.						p.					
	e.						q.					
60.							r.					
61.							s.					
62.							t.					
63.							(other)					
64.	a.											
	b.											

		YES
71.	a.	
	b.	
	c.	
	d.	
	(other)	

65.	a.				
	b.				
66.	a.				
	b.				
67.	a.				
	b.				
	c.				
	d.				
	e.				
	f.				

		YES	NO
72.			
73.			
74.			
75.			
76.			
77.	a.		
	b.		
	c.		
	d.		
	e.		
	f.		
	g.		
	h.		
	i.		

68.	a.				
	b.				
	c.				
69.	a.				
	b.				
	c.				
70.	a.				
	b.				
	c.				
	d.				
	e.				
	f.				
	g.				
	h.				

		YES	NO
78.			
79.	a.		
	b.		
	c.		
	d.		
80.	a.		
	b.		
	c.		
	d.		
	e.		
	f.		
81.	a.		
	b.		
	c.		
	d.		
	e.		
	f.		
	g.		
	h.		
82.	a.		
	b.		
	c.		
83.	a.		
	b.		
	c.		
	d.		
	e.		
84.	a.		
	b.		
	c.		
	d.		
	e.		
	f.		

		YES	NO
	g.		
	h.		
	(other)		

		NO	DEMAND	REGULAR
85.	a.			
	b.			
	c.			
	d.			
	(other)			

	YES	NO
86.		

		NO	DEMAND	REGULAR
87.	a.			
	b.			
	c.			
	d.			
	(other)			

		YES	NO
88.	a.		
	b.		
	c.		
	d.		
89.			

15. May users check out materials and equipment
for use in the classroom and outside the school
as well as in the media center?
(Check only if answer is YES):

	IN MEDIA CENTER ONLY		IN CLASSROOM		OUTSIDE SCHOOL	
	STUDENTS	TEACHERS	STUDENTS	TEACHERS	STUDENTS	TEACHERS
Books	☐	☐	☐	☐	☐	☐
Newspapers	☐	☐	☐	☐	☐	☐
Pamphlet file materials	☐	☐	☐	☐	☐	☐
Periodicals						
Current	☐	☐	☐	☐	☐	☐
Back issues	☐	☐	☐	☐	☐	☐
AV materials	☐	☐	☐	☐	☐	☐
AV equipment	☐	☐	☐	☐	☐	☐
Production materials	☐	☐	☐	☐	☐	☐

43. Does the media center provide the following reference materials
(Check only where answer is YES):

	FOR WHOM		FOR USE IN		
	S	T	MEDIA CENTER	CLASS	OUTSIDE SCHOOL
Basic tools for self-help	☐	☐	☐	☐	☐

	FOR WHOM		FOR USE IN		
	S	T	MEDIA CENTER	CLASS	OUTSIDE SCHOOL
Encyclopedias Other reference tools, e.g. dictionaries, almanacs	☐	☐	☐	☐	☐
Comprehensive tools for self-help, e.g. subject indexes	☐	☐	☐	☐	☐

WORKS CITED

American Association of School Librarians and Association for Educational Communications and Technology. *Media Programs: District and School.* American Library Association and Association for Educational Communications and Technology, 1975.

Blackman, Allan. "The Meaning and Use of Standards," in Henrik L. Blum and others, eds., *Health Planning: Notes on Comprehensive Planning for Health,* p. 4.33–43. School of Public Health, University of California, 1969.

Brutcher, Constance; Gessford, Glen; and Rixford, Emmet. "Cost Accounting for the Library." *Library Resources and Technical Services* 8:413–31 (Fall 1964).

Crookston, Mary E. *Unit Costs in a Selected Group of High School Libraries.* U.S. Office of Education, Bulletin no. 11. Government Printing Office, 1941.

Daniel, Evelyn H. "Performance Measurement for School Libraries," in Melvin J. Voight and Michael H. Harris, eds., *Advances in Librarianship,* vol. 6. Academic Press, to be published in 1976.

DeProspo, Ernest R., and Liesener, James W. "Media Program Evaluation: A Working Framework," *School Media Quarterly* 3:289–301 (Summer 1975).

DeProspo, Ernest R., and Samuels, Alan R. "A Program Planning and Evaluation Self Instructional Manual," in James W. Liesener, ed., *Media Program Evaluation in an Accountability Climate: Proceedings of the AASL Special Program, San Francisco, June 29, 1975.* American Library Association, 1976.

Drott, M. Carl. "Random Sampling: A Tool for Library Research," *College and Research Libraries* 30:119–25 (March 1969).

Fazar, Willard. "Program Planning and Budgeting Theory," *Special Libraries* 60:423–33 (Sept. 1969).

Gaver, Mary V. "Services in Secondary School Media Centers: A Second Appraisal," *School Libraries* 20:15–21 (Fall 1970).

——— *Services of Secondary School Media Centers: Evaluation and Development.* American Library Association, 1971.

——— and Jones, Milbrey. "Secondary Library Services: A Search for Essentials," *Teachers College Record* 68:200–10 (Dec. 1966).

Heinritz, Fred J. "Quantitative Management in Libraries," *College and Research Libraries* 31:232–38 (July 1970).

Henne, Frances; Ersted, Ruth; and Lohrer, Alice. *A Planning Guide for the High School Library Program.* American Library Association, 1951.

Jain, A. K. "Sampling In-Library Book Use," *Journal of the American Society for Information Science* 2:150–55 (May–June 1972).

Jones, William G. "A Time-Series Sample Approach for Measuring Use in a Small Library," *Special Libraries* 64:280–84 (July 1973).

Knezevich, Stephen J. *Program Budgeting (PPBS): A Resource Allocation Decision System for Education.* McCutchan Publishing Corporation, 1973.

Kraft, Donald H., and Liesener, James W. "An Application of a Cost-Benefit Approach to Program Planning: School Media Programs," in *Proceedings of the American Society for Information Science* 10:116–117. American Society for Information Science, 1973.

Liesener, James W. "A Planning Process for School Library/Media Programs," in David R. Bender, ed., *Issues in Media Management,* p. 31–44. Maryland State Department of Education, Division of Library Development and Services, 1973.

———— *District and Regional Learning Resource (Media) Programs: A Systematic Planning Process and Exploratory Survey of Services.* Texas Education Agency, 1975.

———— *Planning Instruments for School Library/ Media Programs.* American Library Association, 1974.

———— "The Development of a Planning Process for Media Programs," *School Media Quarterly* 1:278–87 (Summer 1973).

Liesener, James W., and Levitan, Karen M. *A Process for Planning School Media Programs: Defining Service Outputs, Determining Resource and Operational Requirements, and Estimating Costs.* College of Library and Information Services, University of Maryland, 1972.

Liesener, James W., and Olson, Edwin E. "Survey of User Services in Indiana School Libraries," *Hoosier School Libraries* 8:7–9 (Summer 1969).

Olson, Edwin E. "Development of a General Inventory of Library User Services: Description of Project February 1, 1969 to December 31, 1969." Mimeographed. College of Library and Information Services, University of Maryland, 1970.

———— *Survey of User Service Policies in Indiana Libraries and Information Centers.* Indiana Library Studies, Report no. 10. Indiana State Library, 1970.

———— "Quantitative Approaches to Assessment of Library Service Functions," in James A. Ramey, ed., *Impact of Mechanization on Libraries and Information Centers: Fifth Annual National Colloquium on Information Retrieval,* p. 97–113. Information Interscience, 1968.

———— and Liesener, James W. *An Experimental Educational Program in Library and Information Services: Report no. 1.* College of Library and Information Services, University of Maryland, 1971.

Orr, Richard H. "Measuring the Goodness of Library Services: A General

FORSYTH LIBRARY
FORT HAYS KANSAS STATE COLLEGE

Framework for Considering Quantitative Measures," *Journal of Documentation* 29:328–30 (Sept. 1973).

———— and others. "Development of Methodologic Tools for Planning and Managing Library Services: I. Project Goals and Approach," *Bulletin of the Medical Library Association* 56:235–40 (July 1968).

———— and others. "Development of Methodologic Tools for Planning and Managing Library Services: III. Standardized Inventories of Library Services," *Bulletin of the Medical Library Association* 56:380–403 (Oct. 1968).

Spencer, Carol C. "Random Time Sampling with Self-Observation for Library Cost Studies: Unit Costs of Interlibrary Loans and Photocopies at a Regional Medical Library," *Journal of the American Society for Information Science* 22:153–60 (May–June 1971).

Wedgeworth, Robert. "Budgeting for School Media Centers," *School Libraries* 20:29–36 (Spring 1971).